Industrial Relations

An International and Comparative Bibliography

Industrial Relations

An International and Comparative Bibliography

Compiled by

John Bennett and Julian Fawcett

for the
British Universities Industrial Relations Association

Mansell Publishing Limited, *London and New York*

First published 1985 by Mansell Publishing Limited
(A subsidiary of The H. W. Wilson Company)
6 All Saints Street, London N1 9RL, England
950 University Avenue, Bronx, New York 10452, U.S.A.

British Library Cataloguing in Publication Data

Bennett, John, *1946–*
    Industrial relations: an international and
    comparative bibliography.
    1. Industrial relations—Bibliography
    I. Title   II. Fawcett, Julian   III. British
    Universities Industrial Relations Association
    016.331   Z7164.L1

    ISBN 0–7201–1787–9

Library of Congress Cataloging in Publication Data

Bennett, J. D. (John D.)
    Industrial relations.

    Includes index.
    1. Industrial relations—Bibliography.   I. Fawcett,
Julian.   II. British Universities Industrial
Relations Association.   III. Title.
Z7164.L1B454   1985   [HD6971]   016.331   85–18771

Printed in Great Britain by Henry Ling Limited, Dorchester,
bound by Robert Hartnoll (1985 Ltd), Bodmin, Cornwall

Contents

Foreword

In 1983 the British Universities Industrial Relations Association (BUIRA) recognized the difficulties facing its members in developing comparative studies of industrial relations, and established a Steering Committee charged with producing a wide-ranging and up-to-date bibliography. This book is the product of that initiative, and I am sure it will prove a valuable resource to all those interested in pursuing both teaching and research in industrial relations on a comparative basis.

The bibliography has involved a substantial co-operative effort by many people. The BUIRA is grateful to the University of Warwick, and to Peter Tucker, its Librarian, for the support given to the principal compilers. John Bennett and Julian Fawcett have undertaken the bulk of the work involved in this detailed and complicated task. Elizabeth Wylie, from the Library, assisted with copy preparation, and Iain Liddell, of the University's Computer Unit, guided the work through its mechanized stage. Professor William Brown, as Chairman of the Steering Committee, played a crucial role in guiding the project and in maintaining its impetus to completion—advised and helped from time to time by Steering Committee members, Professor Rod Martin and Dr Paul Willman. Many individual members of the BUIRA, who are acknowledged elsewhere, also assisted with suggestions for inclusion.

It is hoped that as time passes this pioneering work will periodically be brought up to date through future editions.

JOHN GOODMAN
President
British Universities Industrial Relations Association

Introduction

The bibliography's scope is constrained thematically, geographically and chronologically. The subject in the title is industrial relations, though no particular definition of that term has been adopted. This is partly because it was assumed that users of the bibliography would almost certainly have their own definitions, and partly because the term may cover different subject areas in different countries. Broadly, however, material is included on collective bargaining, industrial conflict, the institutions of industrial relations, labour economics, labour history, labour law and the management of labour. Within each country section, the range of material is governed by what is available. Some general works or works outside the area described above may be included for countries on which little has been written. Users of the bibliography, particularly researchers, will perhaps be as interested in the poorly represented nations as in those with a large literature.

An attempt has been made to cover all countries. A little confusion has arisen from time to time over name and boundary changes, and there are some countries on which we have been able to discover no material. In general, the latter are small, often island states, such as Tuvalu or Vanuatu. The compilers would be glad to be informed of works on countries that have been omitted. Some of the general works listed in the International section may include material on some of the missing countries.

We have attempted as far as possible to include mainly works from the last decade. This principle has been breached, however, when an older work is still relevant and is the major or only work in the field, or when the exclusion of older material would leave a country uncovered.

The bibliography contains references to books, journal articles and essays in books of readings. Pamphlets and other small publications are included where relevant and useful. By and large, theses have been excluded, though a few have crept in for countries on which there is little else. The vast majority of the publications cited are held either in the Library of the International Labour Organization in Geneva, or in the University of Warwick Library.

Again as far as possible, English-language publications have been sought. Where necessary, however, works in French, German and Spanish have been included. A few works in other languages have been included, but only where there is an alternative title in English and where a translation or summary in English is available.

The bibliography is arranged hierarchically at three levels: geographical, chronological and alphabetical. In other words, within each country section, works are arranged first in order of the year of publication and then in alphabetical order of authors' names. British Standard BS 5374: 1981 was used as the definitive list of countries and their titles. Several countries in the Caribbean have been coalesced into the 'West Indies', as otherwise most of the material in that area would have appeared in the International section. The subject index will refer readers appropriately. The Steering Committee decided at an early stage that the bibliography shold not include a full section on either the United Kingdom or the United States. This was partly because the literature on those countries is so large that selection would be impossible. Another reason was that good bibliographic materials already exist elsewhere on those countries, and they are listed in the relevant sections.

After each country section, where appropriate, a list of references to other relevant publications, usually in the International section, has been appended. An author index lists the names of all authors, editors and compilers associated with any of the works cited. The subject index includes country names as well as subject keywords. References in both indexes are to entry numbers.

In the case of those sections compiled by the main compilers, the sources consulted were exclusively those available in the University of Warwick Library. The most important single source, particularly for Third World countries, was *International Labour Documentation*.

The following, mostly members of the BUIRA, compiled sections of the bibliography as indicated:

Hugh Roberts, University of East Anglia (Algeria)
Patricia Fosh, Imperial College of Science and Technology (Bolivia and Malaysia)
Gregor Murray, McGill University (Canada)
Ian Boraston, Sheffield Polytechnic (Finland)
Chrys Nassufi, University of Warwick (Greece)
Ian Gow, University of Warwick (Japan)
Paul Worm, Imperial College of Science and Technology (Netherlands)
Chris Leggett, National University of Singapore (Singapore)
Robin Smith, Durham University Business School (South Africa)
Somsong Patarapanich, National University of Singapore (Thailand)
Jon Clark, University of Southampton (West Germany)

We are grateful to the above and to others too numerous to mention for suggestions and advice. Errors and omissions are, of course, entirely our responsibility.

JOHN BENNETT and JULIAN FAWCETT
University of Warwick Library

International

1. International Labour Organisation. *Report on the visit of a joint team of experts on labour-management relations to Pakistan and Ceylon.* Geneva: I.L.O., 1961.

2. Alexander, Robert J. *Labour relations in Argentina, Brazil and Chile.* McGraw-Hill, 1962.

3. Zuzik, Michael B. *Labour law and practice in Malaysia and Singapore.* Washington: U.S.G.P.O., 1965.

4. Frank, Andre Gunder. *Capitalism and underdevelopment in Latin America: historical studies of Chile and Brazil.* New York: Monthly Review Press, 1969.

5. Sommerkorn, Ingrid, Nave-Herz, R. and Kulke, Christine. *Women's careers: experience from East and West Germany.* London: Political and Economic Planning, 1970.

6. Organisation of African Unity. *Occupational health centres in member states of the OAU.* Addis Ababa: O.A.U., 1971. 49p.

7. Witte, A. D. *Employment in the manufacturing sector of developing economies: a study of Mexico, Peru and Venezuela.* Raleigh: Department of Economics, North Carolina State University, 1971. xi, 272p.

8. Central Treaty Organization. *Cento Seminar on Industrial Relations, 1972, Tehran.* Ankara: Cento, 1972. 184p.

9. Coventry and District Engineering Employers' Association. *Labour relations and employment conditions in the European Economic Community.* Coventry: The Association, 1972. 148p.

10. Gunter, H. (ed.) *Transnational industrial relations.* London: Macmillan, 1972.

11. Henry, Z. *Labour relations and industrial conflict in Commonwealth Caribbean countries.* Port-of-Spain: Columbus Publishers, 1972. xii, 283p.

12. Langer, S. *Selected bibliography on the Gambia, Ghana, Liberia, Nigeria and Sierra Leone: economic and social aspects with special reference to labour problems.* Geneva: International Institute for Labour Studies, 1972. vi, 69p.

13. Roberts, B. C. *Future industrial relations: Netherlands, Norway, Sweden and the United Kingdom.* Geneva: International Institute for Labour Studies, 1972. iv, 38p.

14. Sellier, F. *Future industrial relations: France, Italy, Portugal and Spain*. Geneva: International Institute for Labour Studies, 1972. iv, 21p.

15. Stewart, M. *Employment conditions in Europe*. London: Gower, 1972. xviii, 206p.

16. Boyd, T. and French, S. "Summary of research findings on secondary school leaver employment in West Africa, 1969-1971." *Manpower and Unemployment Research in Africa Newsletter*, 6, 1 (April 1973), 56-61.

17. Confederation of British Industry. *Industrial relations and working conditions: Belgium and Luxembourg*. London: C.B.I., 1973. 8p.

18. International Labour Organisation. *Exercise of civil liberties and trade union rights in Angola, Mozambique and Guinea Bissau*. Geneva: I.L.O., 1973. 12p.

19. Nwanza, Z. M. *Modern sector employment growth in East Africa (with special emphasis on Zambia)*. Ithaca: Cornell University, 1973. xiv, 208p.

20. Roberts, B. C. "Multinational collective bargaining: a European prospect." *British Journal of Industrial Relations*, 11, 1 (March 1973), 1-19.

21. Rosner, M., Kavcic, B. and Tannenbaum, A. S. "Workers, participation and influence in five countries." *Industrial Relations*, 12, 2 (May 1973) 200-12.

   Austria, Israel, Italy, USA, Yugoslavia.

22. United Nations. Commission on Human Rights. *Allegations regarding infringements of trade union rights*. New York: U.N., 1973. 58p.

   Angola, Mozambique, Namibia, Zimbabwe.

23. Dore, R. P. *Late development or something else? Industrial relations in Britain, Japan, Mexico, Sri Lanka, Senegal*. Brighton: Sussex University, Institute of Development Studies, 1974. 44p. (Discussion paper 61).

24. Fei, J. C. H. and Ranis, G. *Model of growth and employment in the open dualistic economy: the cases of Korea and Taiwan*. New Haven: Yale Economic Growth Center, 1974. 52p.

25. Guha, S. "Contribution of non-farm activities to rural employment promotion: experience in Iran, India and Syria." *International Labour Review*, 109, 3 (March 1974), 235-50.

26. Hamoudi, Q. *Applications des conventions et récommendations internationales du travail par les états arabes: contribution a la théorie du droit international des relations de travail.* Lille: University of Lille, 1974. iv, 321p.

27. International Labour Organisation and Pakistan. Ministry of Labour, Health, Social Welfare and Population Planning. *National Seminar on Labour-management Relations, 1974.* Islamabad: I.L.O., 1974. ii, 112p.

    Pakistan, Sri Lanka.

28. Lecaillon, J. and Germidis, D. *Disparité de salaires au Senegal, Cameroun, Madagascar et Cote d'Ivoire.* Geneva: I.L.O., 1974. 42p.

29. Levinson, C. *Industry's democratic revolution.* London: Allen & Unwin, 1974. 350p.

    Israel, Yugoslavia and O.E.C.D. countries.

30. Roberts, B. C. "The response of multinational enterprises to international trade union pressures." *British Journal of Industrial Relations*, 12, 3 (November 1974), 403-16.

31. Thuy, N. T. *Population and employment in five selected South Asian countries: a comparative study.* Geneva: International Institute for Labour Studies, 1974. 40p.

    Includes Indonesia and Malaysia.

32. United Nations. Economic Commission for Africa. *Development change and economic policy for employment and training programmes: case studies of Zambia and Botswana.* Addis Ababa: U.N., 1974. v, 80p.

33. International Labour Organisation. *Employers' organisations and industrial relations in Asia.* Geneva: I.L.O., 1975. 254p.

34. Kendall, Walter. *The labour movement in Europe.* London: Allen Lane, 1975.

35. Pakistan. Ministry of Labour and Works. Manpower Division. *Manpower planning: proceedings of a seminar.* Islamabad: The Ministry, 1975. xi, 209p.

    Turkey, Pakistan and Iran.

36. Seidman, Joel. *Industrial relations systems of the United States and New Zealand: a comparison.* Hawaii University, Industrial Relations Center, 1975.

37. Shutt, H. *Worker participation in West Germany, Sweden, Yugoslavia and the United Kingdom.* London: Economist Intelligence Unit, 1975. 48p. (Special report 20).

38. Bomers, G. B. J. *Multinational corporations and industrial relations: a comparative study of West Germany and the Netherlands.* Assen: Van Gorcum, 1976.

39. Carew, Anthony. *Democracy and government in European trade unions.* London: Allen & Unwin, 1976.

40. Clegg, High. *Trade unionism under collective bargaining: a theory based on comparisons of 6 countries.* Oxford: Blackwell, 1976. 121p.

Australia, France, Sweden, U.K., U.S.A., West Germany.

41. Jacobs, W. R. "Trade unionism in multi-racial societies and its impact on the political economy: A comparative analysis of Malaya, Trinidad and Zambia." *Labour and Society,* 1, 1 (January 1976), 79-94.

42. Peek, P. *Education and employment of children: a comparative study of San Salvador and Khartoum.* Geneva: I.L.O., 1976. 22p.

43. Roberts, I. L. "Industrial relations and the European Community." *Industrial Relations Journal,* 7, 2 (Summer 1976), 23-35.

44. Sorge, Arndt. "The evolution of industrial democracy in the countries of the European Community." *British Journal of Industrial Relations,* 14, 3 (November 1976) 274-94.

45. Stewart, Margaret. *Employment conditions in Europe.* Second edition. London: Gower, 1976.

46. Windmuller, John P. "European regionalism: a new factor in international labour." *Industrial Relations Journal,* 7, 2 (Summer 1976), 36-48.

47. Bomers, G. and Peterson, R. "Multinational corporations and industrial relations: the case of West Germany and the Netherlands." *British Journal of Industrial Relations,* 15, 1 (March 1977), 45-62.

48. Carby-Hall, J. R. *Worker participation in Europe.* London: Croom Helm, 1977.

49. Roberts, B. C. "International regulation of multinational enterprises: trade union and management concerns." *British Journal of Industrial Relations,* 15, 3 (November 1977), 356-73.

50. Baffoe, Frank. "Population, manpower and employment in

Southern Africa with special reference to Botswana, Lesotho and Swaziland." *Labour and Society*, 3, 1 (January 1978), 21-44.

51. Bronstein, Arthur S. "Collective bargaining in Latin America: problems and trends." *International Labour Review*, 117 (September-October 1978), 583-96.

52. Coombes, D. "Trade unions and political parties in Britain, France, Italy and West Germany." *Government and Opposition*, 13 (Autumn 1978), 485-95.

53. Crouch, Colin and Pizzorno, Alessandro. *The resurgence of class conflict in Western Europe since 1968.* London: Macmillan, 1978. Two volumes.

54. Enckell, Laurent C. "A trade union perspective on multinational bargaining." Industrial Relations Research Association. *Proceedings,* 1977. New York: I.R.R.A., 1978. 90-96, 105-12.

55. Kassalow, Everett M. "Aspects of labor relations in multinational companies: an overview of three Asian countries." *International Labour Review*, 117, 3 (May-June 1978), 273-87.

Philippines, Malaysia, Singapore.

56. Kassalow, Everett M. "Industrial conflict in comparative perspective." Industrial Relations Research Association. *Proceedings,* 1977. New York: I.R.R.A., 1978. 113-48.

57. King, C. D. and Van de Vall, M. *Models of industrial democracy: consultation, co-determination and workers' management.* The Hague: Moulton, 1978. ix, 218p.

U.K., West Germany and Yugoslavia.

58. Kowet, D. K. *Land, labour migration and politics in Southern Africa: Botswana, Lesotho and Swaziland.* Uppsala: Nordiska Afrikaninstitutet, 1978. 243p.

59. Lansbury, Russell. "Industrial democracy under liberal capitalism: a comparison of trends in Australia, France and the USA." *Journal of Industrial Relations*, 20, 4 (1978), 431-45.

60. McCullough, G. B. "Multinational bargaining: an MNC perspective." Industrial Relations Research Association. *Proceedings,* 1977. New York: I.R.R.A., 1978. 97-112.

61. Murg, Gary E. and Fox, John C. *Labour relations law: Canada, Mexico and Western Europe.* Practising Law Institute, 1978. Two volumes.

62. Ner, A. B. and Neuberger, E. *Israeli kibbutz and the Yugoslav enterprise: a systematic analysis.* New York: New York State University, Stony Brook Department of Economics, 1978. 118p.

63. Porket, J. L. "Industrial relations and participation in management in the Soviet-type communist system." *British Journal of Industrial Relations,* 16, 1 (March 1978), 70-85.

64. Rojot, Jacques. *International collective bargaining: an analysis and case study for Europe.* Kluwer, 1978. 183p.

65. Torrington, Derek (ed.) *Comparative industrial relations in Europe.* Brighton: Greenwood Press, 1978. 269p.

66. Weinberg, Paul. *European labour and multinationals.* New York: Praeger, 1978. 112p.

67. Windmuller, John P. "Some perspectives on multinational bargaining." Industrial relations Research Association. *Proceedings,* 1977. New York: I.R.R.A., 1978. 81-112.

68. Windmuller, John P. and Baderschneider, Jean A. "International guidelines for industrial relations: outlook and impact." Industrial Relations Research Association. *Proceedings,* 1977. New York: I.R.R.A., 1978. 81-9.

69. Adam, J. *Wage control and inflation in the Soviet Bloc countries.* New York: Praeger, 1979. xx, 243p.

U.S.S.R., Poland, Hungary, Czechoslovakia and East Germany.

70. Cohen, Robin, Gutkind, Peter and Brazier, Phyllis. *Peasants and proletarians.* London: Hutchinson, 1979.

71. Coldrick, A. P. and Jones, Philip. *The international directory of the trade union movement.* London: Macmillan, 1979.

72. Cooper, Cary L. and Mumford, Enid. *The quality of working life in Western and Eastern Europe.* London: Associated Business Press, 1979.

73. Damachi, Ukandi G., Seibel, H. Dieter and Trachtman, Lester (eds.) *Industrial relations in Africa.* New York: St. Martin's Press, 1979. 373p.

74. International Labour Organisation. *Egalité de chances et de traitement en matière emploi: le role de l'infrastructure sociale dans les pays de l'Europe de l'Est.* Geneva: I.L.O., 1979. 85p.

75. International Labour Organisation. *Role of employers' associations in the arab countries: proceedings of a round table.* Geneva: I.L.O., 1979.

76. Kendall, P. M. H., Crayston, J., Malecki, A. M. J. and Wallace, A. S. *Impact of chip technology on employment and the labour market.* The Hague: Ministerie von Sociale Zaken, 1979. iv, 415.

France, Norway, U.K. and West Germany.

77. La Palombara, J. G. and Blank, S. *Multinational corporations and developing countries.* New York: Conference Board, 1979. 215p.

78. Maurice, M. "A societal analysis of industrial relations: a comparison between France and West Germany." *British Journal of Industrial Relations,* 17, 3 (November 1979), 322-36.

79. Peil, M. "West African urban craftsmen." *Journal of Developing Areas,* 14, 1 (October 1979), 3-22.

80. Organisation for Economic Co-operation and Development. *Wage policies and collective bargaining developments in Finland, Ireland and Norway.* Paris: O.E.C.D., 1979.

81. Roberts, B. C. (ed.) *Towards industrial democracy.* London: Osmun, 1979. 287p.

82. Seminar on Collective Bargaining and Labour Arbitration in South Asia, Colombo, 1978. *Proceedings.* Bangkok: Friedrich-Ebert-Stiftung, 1979. 182p.

Bangladesh, India, Nepal, Pakistan, Sri Lanka.

83. Bain, George S. and Price, Robert. *Profiles of union growth.* Oxford: Blackwell, 1980. 177p.

84. Ernst, Dieter. *The new international division of labour.* Berlin: Campus, 1980.

85. Frobel, Folker, Heinrichs, Jurgen and Kreze, Otto. *The new international division of labour.* Cambridge: Cambridge University Press, 1980. 407p.

86. Galin, Amira. "Aspects of compulsory intervention in Australia and Israel." *Journal of Industrial Relations,* 22 (March 1980), 19-35.

87. International Labour Organisation. *Report of the ILO/DANIDA Advance Mission of Trade Union and Co-operative activities, 1980.* Geneva: I.L.O., 1980. 20p.

Uganda, Tanzania and Zambia.

88. International Labour Organisation. *Work and family life: the role of the social infrastructure in Eastern European countries.* Geneva: I.L.O., 1980. vi, 77p.

Hungary, Poland, East Germany, Czechoslovakia and U.S.S.R.

89. Jones, Derek C. "Producer co-operatives in industrialised western economies." *British Journal of Industrial Relations,* 18, 2 (July 1980), 141-54.

90. Levine, S. B. "Changing strategies of unions and management: evaluation of four industrialised countries." *British Journal of Industrial Relations,* 18, 1 (March 1980), 70-81.

Japan, Australia, Singapore, U.K.

91. Liebhaberg, Bruno. *Industrial relations and multinational corporations in Europe.* London: Gower, 1980.

92. Reynaud, Jean-Daniel. "Industrial relations and political systems: some reflections on the crisis in industrial relations in Western Europe." *British Journal of Industrial Relations,* 18, 1 (March 1980), 1-13.

93. Rowan, Richard L., Northrup, Herbert R. and O'Brien, Rae Ann. *Multinational union organisations in the manufacturing industries.* University of Pennsylvania, Wharton School, Industrial Research Unit, 1980. 213p.

94. Windmuller, John P. *The international trade union movement.* Kluwer, 1980. 174p.

95. Wright, Michael and Apple, Nixon. "Incomes policy and industrial relations: Britain, Sweden and Australia." *Journal of Industrial Relations,* 22, 4 (1980), 453-75.

96. Zwerdling, D. *Workplace democracy: a guide to workplace ownership, participation and self-management experiments in the United States and Europe.* New York: Harper Colophon, 1980. xii, 195p.

U.S., Spain, Yugoslavia and U.K.

97. Anderson, Gordon. "Industrial relations in smaller countries." *New Zealand Journal of Industrial Relations,* 6, 3 (December 1981), 121-4.

98. Bennell, P. S. "Earnings differentials between public and private sectors in Africa: the cases of Ghana, Kenya and Nigeria." *Labour and Society,* 6, 3 (July-September 1981), 223-41.

99. Chamot, D. and Dymmel, M. D. *Co-operation or conflict: European experiences with technological change at the workplace.* Washington: A.F.L.-C.I.O., Department for Professional Employees, 1981. 32p.

U.K., Norway, Sweden, West Germany.

100. Defrien, J. M. *Conditions de travail et sous-développement: les industries agro-alimentaires au Senegal et au Togo.* Paris: Editions C.N.R.S., 1981. 296p.

101. Doeringer, P. *Industrial relations in international perspective: essays on research and policy.* New York: Holmes & Meier, 1981. 425p.

102. Hare, P. G. and Wanless, P. J. "Polish and Hungarian economic reforms: a comparison." *Soviet Studies*, 33 (October 1981), 491-507.

103. Industrial Democracy in Europe. International Research Group. *European industrial relations.* Oxford: Oxford University Press, 1981. 277p.

104. Industrial Democracy in Europe. International Research Group. *Industrial democracy in Europe.* Oxford: Clarendon Press, 1981. 449p.

105. Institute of Social Studies, The Hague and Indian Institute of Management. *Industrial democracy and development: building on experience.* The Hague: The Institute, 1981. vii, 112p.

Tanzania and Sri Lanka.

106. International Labour Organisation. *Field experiments in new forms of work organisation: India, Tanzania: project findings.* Geneva: I.L.O., 1981. iii, 73p.

107. International Labour Organisation. Jobs and Skills Programme for Africa. *Problèmes d'emploi et de formation au programme de l'Organisation pour la mise en valeur du Fleuve Senegal.* Addis Ababa: I.L.O., 1981. 127p.

Mali, Mauritania and Senegal.

108. International Labour Organisation. Meeting of Experts on Household Surveys, Geneva, 1981. *Highlights from labour force surveys in African countries.* Geneva: I.L.O., 1981. 5p.

Kenya, Lesotho and Morocco.

109. International Labour Organisation. *Planification des résources humaines et information sur le marché de l'emploi: résultats de missions dans cinq pays d'Afrique noire et d'Afrique du Nord.* Geneva: I.L.O., 1981. 24p.

Congo, Morocco, Togo, Tunisia and Zaire.

110. International Labour Organisation. *Report of the Tripartite Workshop on Labour Relations, Nairobi, 1981.* Geneva: I.L.O., 1981. 36p.

Kenya, Tanzania, Zambia and Zimbabwe.

111. Kanawaty, G., Thorsrud, E., Semicuo, J. P. and Singh, J. P. "Field experiments with new forms of work organisation." *International Labour Review,* 120, 3 (May-June 1981), 263-77.

India and Tanzania.

112. Knight, J. B. "Labour markets in developing countries." *Oxford Bulletin of Economics and Statistics,* 43, 1 (February 1981), 1-111.

Bangladesh, India, Kenya and Tanzania.

113. Lindley, R. M., Kruseman, J. L., Capron, H. and Schoon, A. *International comparison of the effects of public expenditure on employment: Belgium, France and the United Kingdom.* Brussels: European Communities, 1981.

114. Poole, Michael. *Theories of trade unionism.* London: Routledge & Kegan Paul, 1981.

115. Psacharopoulos, G. "Education, employment and inequality in less developed countries." *World Development,* 9 (January 1981), 37-54.

116. Schregle, Johannes. "Comparative industrial relations: pitfalls and potential." *International Labour Review,* 120, 1 (January-February 1981), 15-30.

117. Sethi, K. C., Sengupta, A. K., Grozdanic, S. S. and Stambuk, V. *Self-management and workers' participation: Indo-Yugoslav experience.* New Delhi: Scope, 1981. lvi, 598p.

118. Smith, D. "Testing a behavioural theory of bargaining: an international study." *British Journal of Industrial Relations,* 19, 3 (November 1981), 361-9.

New Zealand and U.S.A.

119. Triska, Jan F. and Gati, Charles (eds.) *Blue collar workers in Eastern Europe.* London: Allen & Unwin, 1981. 302p.

120. Tse, C. *Invisible control: management control of workers in a U.S. electronic company with reference to Hong Kong and Korea.* Hong Kong: Centre for the Progress of Peoples, 1981. iii, 70p.

121. Williams, S. *Youth without work: three countries approach the problem.* Paris: O.E.C.D., 1981. 255p.

Denmark, U.S.A. and West Germany.

122. Windmuller, John P. "Concentration trends in union structure: an international comparison." *Industrial and Labor Relations Review,* 35 (October 1981), 43-57.

123. Adam, J. *Employment policies in the Soviet Union and Eastern Europe.* London: Macmillan, 1982. xvii, 216p.

124. Blanpain, R. (ed.) *Comparative labour law and industrial relations.* Kluwer, 1982. 411p.

125. Bratt, Christian. *Labour relations in seventeen countries.* Swedish Employers' Confederation, 1982. 134p.

126. Buck, Trevor W. *Comparative industrial systems.* London: St. Martin's Press, 1982. 177p.

127. Cooper, M. R. *Search for consensus: the role of institutional dialogue between government, labour and employers: the experience of five countries.* Paris: O.E.C.D., 1982. 77p.

France, Netherlands, Norway and West Germany.

128. Dixon, R. B. "Mobilizing women for rural employment in South Asia: issues of class, caste and patronage." *Economic Development and Cultural Change,* 30, 2 (January 1982), 373-90.

Bangladesh, India, Nepal and Pakistan.

129. Drazen, A. "Unemployment in less developed countries." *World Development,* 10 (December 1982), 1039-47.

130. Galin, A. and Lansbury, R. "Wage indexation and industrial relations: a comparison of recent experience in Israel and Australia." *New Zealand Journal of Industrial Relations,* 7, 1 (April 1982), 13-22.

131. Giddens, Anthony and Mackenzie, Gavin (eds.) *Social class and division of labour.* Cambridge: Cambridge University Press, 1982.

132. Industrial Relations Services. "Terms and conditions at International Harvester." *European Industrial Relations Review,* 98 (March 1982), 13-17.

France, Spain, U.K. and West Germany.

133. International Labour Organisation. *Labour market information through key informants: report of an evaluation seminar.* Geneva:

I.L.O., 1982. ii, 85p.

Antigua, Bangladesh, India, Malaysia, Nepal, Sri Lanka and Thailand.

134. International Labour Organisation. *Labour relations and development: country studies on Japan, the Philippines, Singapore and Sri Lanka.* Geneva: I.L.O., 1982. 153p.

135. International Labour Organisation. Jobs and Skills Programme for Africa. *Manpower demand and supply in the agricultural sector of member states of the Maro River Union.* Addis Ababa: I.L.O., 1982.

Guinea, Liberia and Sierra Leone.

136. Lange, Peter M., Ross, George and Vannicelli, Maurizio. *Unions, change and crisis: French and Italian union strategy and the political economy, 1945-1980.* London: Allen & Unwin, 1982. 295p.

137. Lowit, T. "The working class and union structures in Eastern Europe." *British Journal of Industrial Relations,* 20, 1 (March 1982), 67-75.

138. Schregle, Johannes. *Negotiating development: labour relations in Southern Asia.* Geneva: I.L.O., 1982. 186p.

139. United Nations. Commission on Transnational Corporations. *Transnational corporations in Southern Africa.* New York: U.N., 1982.

140. Walsh, K. "An analysis of strikes in four EEC countries." *Industrial Relations Journal,* 13, 4 (Winter 1982), 65-72.

France, Italy, U.K. and West Germany.

141. Abdin, R., Benneil, P., Fajana, O. and Godfrey, M. *World of differentials: African pay structures in a transnational context.* London: Hodder & Stoughton, 1983. 152p.

Egypt, Ghana, Morocco, Nigeria, Sudan and Tanzania.

142. Barkin, Solomon. *Worker militancy and its consequences.* Second edition. New York: Praeger, 1983.

143. Busch, Gary K. *The political role of international trade unions.* New York: St. Martin's Press, 1983. 287p.

144. Gibbs, C. W. *Needs and opportunities for developing accountants in Southern Africa: Botswana, Lesotho, Malawi, Swaziland and Zambia.* Geneva: I.L.O., 1983. 65p.

145. Hart, G. *Agrarian labor arrangements and structural change:*

concepts and evidence from Java and Bangladesh. Boston: Boston University, Department of Economics, 1983. 105p.

146. International Labour Organisation. *Labour-management relations in public enterprises in Africa.* Geneva: I.L.O., 1983. 84p.

147. International Labour Organisation. *Report on Tripartite Seminar on International Labour Standards for English-speaking countries of Southern Africa.* Geneva: I.L.O., 1983. 7p.

Malawi, Swaziland, Zambia and Zimbabwe.

148. International Labour Organisation and Danish International Development Agency. *Interregional project on promotion and development of workers' education institutions: mission report.* Geneva: I.L.O., 1983. 7p.

Cameroun, Gambia, Liberia, Nigeria, Sierra Leone.

149. Mundle, S. *Labour absorption in agriculture and the restricted market for manufacturing industry: some contrasts between India, Indonesia and Japan.* Trivandrum: Centre for Development Studies, 1983. 28p.

150. Shalev, Michael. "Strikes and the crisis: industrial conflict and unemployment in the Western nations." *Economic and Industrial Democracy,* 4 (November 1983), 417-60.

151. Singleton, W. T. "Occupational safety and health systems: a three-country comparison." *International Labour Review,* 122, 2 (March-April 1983), 155-68.

Includes Switzerland.

152. Sturmthal, Adolf. *Left of centre: European labor since World War II.* Urbana: University of Illinois Press, 1983. 302p.

153. United Nations. Economic and Social Commision for Asia and the Pacific. "Young women in export-orientated manufacturing industries." *Social Development Newsletter,* 9 (December 1983), 22-9.

Philippines, Singapore and Sri Lanka.

154. Vivekanda, F. "Critical unemployment situation in the Nordic countries: alternative strategies for full employment by the year 2000." *Scandinavian Journal of Development Alternatives,* 11, 4 (December 1983), 84-95.

Denmark, Finland, Norway and Sweden.

155. Wilczynski, Josef. *Comparative industrial relations*. London: Macmillan, 1983.

156. Willard, J. C. "France en position médiane pour les couts salariaux." *Eáconomie et Statistique*, 156 (June 1983), 25-41.

Includes material on Belgium and Denmark.

157. Maurice, M., Sellier, P. and Silvestre, J. "Rules, contexts and actors: observations based on a comparison between France and Germany." *British Journal of Industrial Relations*, 22, 3 (November 1984), 346-63.

158. Ramos, Elias T. "Labour policy change and its impact on trade union roles in Singapore and the Philippines: a comparative study." *Indian Journal of Industrial Relations*, 19, 3 (January 1984), 331-46.

159. Windmuller, John P. and Gladstone, Alan, (eds.) *Employers' associations and industrial relations: a comparative study*. Oxford: Clarendon Press, 1984. 370p.

160. Bean, Ron. *Comparative industrial relations: an introduction to cross-national perspectives*. London: Croom Helm, 1985.

Afghanistan

161 United States. Bureau of Labor Statistics. *Labor law and practice in Afghanistan.* Washington: U.S.G.P.O., 1969. 23p.

162. Gerken, E. *Land productivity and the employment problem of rural areas.* New Haven: Yale University, Economic Growth Center, 1973. 36p.

163. Scoville, J. G. "Afghan labor markets: a model of interdependence." *Industrial Relations,* 13, 3 (October 1974), 274-87.

164. Bhathy, I. Z. and Berouti, L. "Development strategy for Afghanistan: lessons of an employment policy mission." *Pakistan Development Review,* 19, 4 (Winter 1980), 337-52.

Albania

165. Albanian Life. "The exploitation of the Albanian peasant at the beginning of the twentieth century." *Albanian Life,* 5 (Autumn 1977), 30-37.

166. Canko, Nesim. "Retirement pensions in Albania." *Albanian Life,* 18 (July 1981), 12-13.

167. Toci, Veniamin. "The transformation of urban craft co-operatives into state property (1968-69)." *Albanian Life,* 20, 1 (1982), 35-6.

168. Day, Steve. "The labour code." *Albanian Life,* 27, 4 (1983), 35-6.

169. Bland, William. "The trade unions of Albania." *Albanian Life,* 29, 2 (1984), 26-9.

170. Bollano, Priamo. "The limitation of wage differentials." *Albanian Life,* 29, 2 (1984), 21-2.

171. Bollano, Priamo and Dari, Fari. "The transition to state farming." *Albanian Life,* 28, 1 (1984), 15-16.

172. Mutrushi, Vasil. "Pensions in Albania." *Albanian Life,* 30, 3 (1984), 21-2.

Algeria

173. Bourdieu, Pierre, Darbel, A., Rivet, J.-P., and Seibel, C. *Travail et travailleurs en Algérie.* Paris and The Hague: Mouton, 1963. 566p.

174. Favret, Jean. "Le syndicat, les travailleurs et le pouvoir en Algérie." *Annuaire de l'Afrique du Nord,* 1964. Paris: C.N.R.S., 1965.

175. Laks, Monique. *Autogestion ouvrière et pouvoir politique en Algérie (1962-1965).* Paris: Etudes et Documentation Internationales, 1970. 335p.

176. Weiss, Francois. *Doctrine et action syndicales en Algérie.* Paris: Editions Cujas, 1970. 363p.

177. Chaulet, Claudine. *La Mitidja autogérée.* Algiers, S.N.E.D., 1971. 402p.

178. Clegg, Ian. *Workers' self-management in Algeria.* London: Penguin, 1971. 249p.

179. Miaille, Michel. "Contribution á une réflexion théoretique sur l'entreprise socialiste en Algérie." *Revue Algérienne des Sciences Juridiques, Economiques et Politiques,* 9, 3 (September 1972), 653-693.

180. Duprat, Gerard. *Révolution et autogestion rurale en Algérie.* Paris: Fondation Nationale des Sciences Politiques - Librairie Armand Colin, 1973. 486p.

181. Helié, Damien. "Industrial self-management in Algeria." Zartman, I. William (ed.) *Man, state and society in the contemporary Maghrib.* London: Pall Mall Press, 1973. p.465-74.

182. Barak, Michel. "Quelques remarques á propos d'une "Contribution á réflexion théorique sur l'entreprise socialiste en Algérie." *Revue Algérienne des Sciences Juridiques, Economiques et Politiques,* 11, 2 (June 1974), 259-98.

183. Koulytchizky, Serge. *L'autogestion, l'homme et l'état: l'expérience algérienne.* Paris and The Hague: Mouton, 1974. 482p.

184. Miaille, Michel. "Réflexion sur une contribution théoretique concernant l'entreprise socialiste algérienne: réponse á quelques remarques." *Revue Algérienne des Sciences Juridiques, Economiques et Politiques,* 11, 2 (June 1974), 299-335.

185. Nellis, John R. *Workers' participation in Algeria's nationalized industries: la gestion socialiste des entreprises.* Ottawa: Carleton University, School of International Affairs, 1976. (Occasional paper 30).

186. Nellis, John R. "Socialist management in Algeria." *Journal of Modern African Studies,* 15, 4 (1977), 529-54.

187. Raffinot, Marc and Jacquemot, Pierre. *Le capitalisme d'état* *algérien.* Paris: François Maspero, 1977. 394p.

188. Boutefnouchet, Mostefa. *Le socialisme dans l'entreprise.* Algiers: Editions En. A.P., 1978.

189. Said-Amer, Tayeb. *L'industrialisation en Algérie: l'entreprise algérienne dans le développement.* Paris: Editions Anthropos, 1978. 264p.

190. Roberts, Hugh. "Is Algeria socialist?" *Gazelle Review of Literature on the Middle East,* 8 (Winter 1980), 1-10.

191. Roberts, Hugh. "The Algerian bureaucracy." Asad, Talal and Owen, Roger (eds.) *Sociology of "developing societies": the Middle East.* London: Macmillan, 1983. p.95-114.

Angola

192. International Labour Organisation. *Participation des travailleurs aux decisions dans l'entreprise en Angola.* Geneva: I.L.O., 1981. 12p.

193. International Labour Organisation. *Rapport au Gouvernement de la République Populaire d'Angola sur les travaux de la Mission Multidisciplinaire du PIACT.* Geneva: I.L.O., 1982. vi, 144p.

Inspection of and recommendations on working conditions.

See also 18, 22.

Argentina

194. Galarza, Ernesto. *Argentine labor under Peron.* Washington: Inter-American Reports, 1948. 15p.

195. Fillol, Tomas Roberto. *Social factors in economic development: the Argentine case.* MIT Press, 1961.

196. Baily, S. L. *Labor, nationalism and politics in Argentina.* Rutgers University Press, 1967. 241p.

197. United Nations. Economic Commission for Latin America. *Economic development and income distribution in Argentina.* New York: U.N., 1969. 269p.

198. Nogues, J. "Alternative trade strategies and employment in the Argentine manufacturing sector." *World Development,* 11 (December 1983), 1029-42.

199. Lagos, R. and Tokman, V. "Monetarism, employment and social stratification." *World Development,* 12 (January 1984), 43-65.

See also 2.

Australia

200. Walker, Kenneth F. *Australian industrial relations systems.* Harvard University Press, 1970.

201. Hancock, Keith. "The occupational wage structure in Australia since 1914." *British Journal of Industrial Relations*, 10, 1 (March 1972), 107-22.

202. Martin, Ross. *Trade unions in Australia.* Harmondsworth, Penguin, 1975.

203. Niland, John and Isaac, J. E. (eds.) *Australian labour economics.* Second edition. Sun, 1975.

204. Cupper, Les. "Legalism in the Australian Conciliation and Arbitration Commission: the gradual transition." *Journal of Industrial Relations*, 18, 4 (1976), 337-64.

205. Dufty, N. F. "Trade unions and their operations." *Journal of Industrial Relations*, 18, 3 (1976), 203-19.

206. Pritchard, Robert L. (ed.) *Industrial democracy in Australia.* CCH, 1976.

207. Simpson, R. C. "The significance of the legal status of trade unions in Britain and Australia." *Journal of Industrial Relations*, 18, 3 (September 1976), 229-42.

208. Bordow, Allan. *The worker in Australia.* University of Queensland Press, 1977.

209. Dunkley, G. and Donn, C. "The founding of the ACTU." *Journal of Industrial Relations*, 19, 4 (1977), 404-23.

210. Farrell, Frank. "The Pan-Pacific trade union movement and Australian labour 1921-1932." *Historical Studies*, 17 (October 1977), 441-57.

211. Gurdon, Michael. "Patterns of industrial relations research in Australia." *Journal of Industrial Relations*, 20, 4 (1978), 446-62.

212. Lansbury, Russell. "Industrial democracy through participation in management: the Australian experience." *Industrial Relations Journal*, 9, 2 (Summer 1978), 71-9.

213. Niland, John. *Collective bargaining and compulsory arbitration in Australia.* New South Wales University Press, 1978.

214. Rawson, D. W. *Unions and unionists in Australia.* Sydney: Allen & Unwin, 1978.

215. Hancock, K. "The first half-century of Australian wage policy." *Journal of Industrial Relations*, 21, 1 (1979), 1-19; 21, 2 (1979), 129-60.

216. McKinley, B. J. *A documentary history of the Australian labour movement.* Drummond, 1979.

217. Boreham, Paul and Dow, Geoff, (eds.) *Work and inequality.* Sydney: Macmillan, 1980.

218. Brown, William. "Occupational pay structures under different wage fixing arrangements: a comparison of intr-occupational pay dispersion in Australia, Great Britain and the United States." *British Journal of Industrial Relations*, 18, 2 (July 1980), 217-30.

219. Cupper, Les. "Public funded trade union education in Australia." *Industrial Relations Journal*, 11, 1 (March-April 1980), 57-68.

220. Dabscheck, Braham. "The Australian model of industrial relations: an analytical model." *Journal of Industrial Relations*, 22, 2 (1980), 196-218.

221. Frenkel, S. J. (ed.) *Industrial action: patterns of labour conflict.* Sydney: Allen & Unwin, 1980.

222. Lansbury, Russell. "Australian white collar unionism in transition." *Industrial Relations Journal*, 10, 4 (Winter 1979-80), 31-42.

223. Plowman, D., Deery, S. and Fisher, C. *Australian industrial relations.* McGraw-Hill, 1980.

224. Crawford, Bob and Volard, Sam. "Work absence in industrialised societies: the Australian case." *Industrial Relations Journal*, 12, 3 (May-June 1981), 50-57.

225. Creighton, B. "Secondary boycotts under attack: the Australian experience." *Modern Law Review*, 44 (September 1981), 489-515.

226. Dabscheck, Braham. "Theories of regulation and Australian industrial relations." *Journal of Industrial Relations*, 23, 4 (1981), 430-46.

227. Dabscheck, Braham and Niland, John. *Industrial relations in Australia.* Sydney: Allen & Unwin, 1981.

228. Hicks, John. "Industrial relations in Australia." *New Zealand Journal of Industrial Relations*, 6 (April 1981), 21-7.

229. Niland, John. "Research and reform in industrial relations." *Journal of Industrial Relations*, 23, 4 (1981), 482-503.

230. Rimmer, Malcolm. "Long-run structural change in Australian trade unionism." *Journal of Industrial Relations*, 23, 3 (1981), 323-43.

231. Rimmer, Malcolm and Sutcliffe, Paul. "The origins of Australian workshop organisation." *Journal of Industrial Relations*, 23, 2 (1981), 216-39.

232. Benson, John. "Trade union attitudes to job sharing in Australia." *Industrial Relations Journal* 13, 3 (Autumn 1982), 13-19.

233. Bray, Mark and Davis, Edward. "Trade union democracy from the inside." *Industrial Relations Journal*, 13, 4 (Winter 1982), 84-93.

234. Deery, S. "Trade unions, technological change and redundancy protection in Australia." *Journal of Industrial Relations*, 24, 2 (1982), 155-75.

235. Dickenson, Mary. *Democracy in trade unions.* University of Queensland Press, 1982.

236. Plowman, D. "Indexation and beyond: Australian wage determination 1978-1982." *New Zealand Journal of Industrial Relations*, 7, 3 (December 1982), 189-204.

237. Waters, Malcolm. *Strikes in Australia.* Sydney: Allen & Unwin, 1982.

238. Ford, Bill and Plowman, David. *Australian unions: an industrial relations perspective.* Sydney: Macmillan, 1983.

239. Ford, G. W., Hearn, J. and Lansbury, R. (eds.) *Australian labour relations: readings.* Third edition. Sydney: Macmillan, 1983.

240. Griffin, Gerry. "White collar unionism 1969-1981: some determinants of growth." *Journal of Industrial Relations*, 25, 1 (1983), 26-37.

241. Howard, William A. "Centralism and perception of Australian industrial relations." *Journal of Industrial Relations*, 25, 1 (1983), 3-25.

242. Rawson, D. W. "British and Australian labour law: the background to the 1982 Bills." *British Journal of Industrial Relations*, 21, 2 (July 1983), 161-80.

243. Hayles, J., Hughes, B. and Rowe, L. "Product and labour markets in wage determination." *British Journal of Industrial Relations*, 22, 2 (July 1984), 169-76.

244. Plowman, David. "Full circle: Australian wage determination 1982-1984." *New Zealand Journal of Industrial Relations*, 9 (August 1984), 95-112.

See also 40, 59, 86, 90, 95, 130.

Austria

245. Barbash, J. and Barbash, K. *Trade unions and national economic policy.* Baltimore: Johns Hopkins Press, 1972. 206p.

246. Guenter, H. *Future industrial relations: FRG and Austria.* Geneva: International Institute for Labour Studies, 1972. iv, 34p.

247. Jahoda, M., Lazarsfeld, P. F. and Zeisel, H. Marienthal. *The sociology of an unemployed community.* London: Tavistock, 1972. xvi, 128p.

248. Kassalow, E. M. *What happens when everyone organises?* Madison: Wisconsin University, Industrial Relations Research Institute, 1972. 6p.

249. United Nations. Economic Commission for Europe. Conference of European Statisticians. *Comparison of levels of labour productivity in industry in Austria...* New York: U.N., 1972. ii, 29p.

250. Rosner, M., Kavcic, B. and Tannenbaum, A. S. "Worker participation and influence." *Industrial Relations,* 12, 2 (May 1973), 200-212.

251. Krebs, E. "Women workers and the trade unions in Austria: an interim report." *International Labour Review,* 112, 4 (October 1975), 265-78.

252. Mire, J. *Country labour profile: Austria.* Washington: U.S.G.P.O., 1979. 7p.

253. Austria. Bundesministerium fuer Soziale Verwaltung. *Women and industrial relations: Austria's national machinery.* Vienna: B.S.V., 1980. 10p.

254. Blattner, N. *Review of selected national reports on the employment impact of microelectronics.* Basel: Institut fuer Angewndte Wirtschaftsforschung, 1981. 38p.

255. International Labour Organisation. *Workers' participation in decisions within undertakings in Austria.* Geneva: I.L.O., 1981. 9p.

256. Industrial Relations Services. "Austria: flexible working hours trends." *European Industrial Relations Review,* 119 (December 1983), 23-4.

257. Lauber, W., Retzer, K. and Schwarz, B. *Leitrader fuer Betriebsvereinbaringen.* Vienna: Osterreichischer Gewerkschaftsbund,

1983. 455p.

258.   Cerny,   J.   *Urlaubsrecht.*   Vienna: Osterreichischer
Gewerkschaftsbund, 1984. 217p.

See also 21.

Bahamas

259. Bahamas. Department of Statistics. *Manpower and income.* Nassau, 1973. 87p.

260. Salt, A. *Bahamas: Manpower aspects of the proposed First Development Plan.* Geneva: I.L.O., 1975. iii, 88p.

Bahrain

261. Bu-Ali, A. R. "Hospital management and management training in Bahrain." *World Hospitals,* 17 (August 1981), 13-14.

Bangladesh

262. Khan, A. A. *Labour and industrial law.* Dacca: Koshroz Kitab Mahal, 1974. viii, 401p.

263. International Labour Organisation. Asian Regional Team for Employment Promotion. *Employment in Bangladesh during the second five-year plan.* Bangkok: I.L.O., 1979. 70p.

264. Siddiqui, Amah. *Labour relations and national development: a case study of Bangladesh.* Bangkok: I.L.O., 1980. 20p.

265. Ahmed, Iqbal. "Wage determination in Bangladesh agriculture." *Oxford Economic Papers,* 33, 2 (July 1981), 298-322.

266. Azim, S. A. *Workers' partnership in decision-making in undertakings in Bangladesh.* Geneva: I.L.O., 1981. 8p.

267. International Labour Organisation. Asian Regional Team for Employment Promotion. *Manpower planning in Bangladesh.* Bangkok: I.L.O., 1981. 140p.

268. Ahmad, M. "Workers' participation: a framework for analysis." *Journal of Management, Business and Economics,* 8, 1 (January 1982), 103-15.

269. Bangladesh. Bureau of Statistics. *Manpower situation in contemporary Bangladesh.* Dacca: The Bureau, 1982. ii, 58p.

270. Bangladesh. Ministry of Labour. *[Proceedings of the] First National Tripartite Labour Conference, 1981.* Dacca: I.L.O., 1982. 77p.

271. Bangladesh Employers' Association. *Proceedings of the Seminar on Productivity, 1982.* Dacca: I.L.O., 1982. 68p.

272. International Labour Organisation. Office in Bangladesh. *Industrial relations laws, policies and principles: compilation of lecture notes for use in the industrial relations institutes.* Dacca: I.L.O., 1982.

273. Masum, M. *Unemployment and underemployment in agriculture: a case study of Bangladesh.* Delhi: B.R. Publishing Corporation, 1982. xii, 264p.

274. Sinniger, J. "Employment situation in Bangladesh." *Bangladesh and ILO Co-operation for Development,* 3 (August 1982), 27-34.

275. Gill, G. "Mechanised land preparation, productivity and employment in Bangladesh." *Journal of Development Studies,* 19 (April 1983), 329-48.

See also 82, 112, 128, 133, 145.

Belgium

276. Seyfarth, Shaw. Fairweather and Geraldson. *Labour relations and the law in Belgium and the United States: a comparative study.* University of Michigan, Graduate School of Business Administration, 1969. 455p.

277. Blanpain, Roger. *Public employee unionism in Belgium.* Ann Arbor: University of Michigan, 1971. 99p.

278. Coates, Ken (ed.) *A trade union strategy in the Common Market: the programme of the Belgian trade unions.* Nottingham: Spokesman, 1971. 149p.

279. Organisation for Economic Co-operation and Development. *Manpower policy in Belgium.* Paris: O.E.C.D., 1971. 187p.

280. Vanachter, O. "Labour relations in Belgium: 1970 survey." *Instituut voor Arbeidsrecht,* 2 (1971), 241-5.

281. Albeda, W. *Participation in management.* Rotterdam: University Press, 1973. 104p.

282. Confederation of British Industry. *Industrial relations and working conditions: Belgium and Luxembourg.* London: C.B.I., 1973. 8p.

283. Blanpain, Roger. "Influence of labour on management decision-making: a comparative legal survey." *Industrial Law Journal,* 3, 1 (March 1974), 5-19.

284. Stearns, P. N. *Lives of labour: work in a maturing industrial* *society*. London: Croom Helm, 1975. viii, 424p.

285. Blanpain, Roger. *The Badger case and the OECD guidelines for multinational enterprises*. Deventer: Kluwer, 1977. 210p.

286. Gevers. P. *Du conseil d'entreprise au conseil des travailleurs? Un dilemme posé au mouvement ouvrier belge*. Antwerp: Universiteit Antwerpen, 1977. 19p.

287. Colens, A. and Colens, M. *Contrat d'emploi: contrat de travail des employés*. Bruxelles: Ferdinand Loucier. 1980. xxviii, 458p.

288. European Foundation for the Improvement of Living and Working Conditions. *Safety and health at the workplace: Belgium*. Dublin: The Foundation, 1980.

289. European Foundation for the Improvement of Living and Working Conditions. *Shiftwork in the chemical industry: case studies of innovations: Belgium*. Dublin: The Foundation, 1981.

290. European Foundation for the Improvement of Living and Working Conditions. *Shiftwork in the chemical industry: surveys: Belgium*. Dublin: The Foundation, 1981.

291. European Foundation for the Improvement of Living and Working Conditions. *Shiftwork in the services sector: Belgium*. Dublin: The Foundation, 1981.

292. Industrial Relations Services. "Belgium: bargaining within a strict framework." *European Industrial Relations Review*, 90 (July 1981), 16-18.

293. Industrial Relations Services. "Belgium: new rights for part-time workers." *European Industrial Relations Review*, 93 (October 1981), 6-7.

294. Industrial Relations Services. "Belgium: premium payments, a review." *European Industrial Relations Review*, 94 (November 1981), 21-2.

295. Industrial Relations Services. "Belgium: redundancy law and practice." *European Industrial Relations Review*, 89 (June 1981), 9-10.

296. Piere, M. "Recent developments in the humanisation of working conditions in Belgium." *International Labour Review*, 120, 3 (May-June 1981), 279-290.

297. European Foundation for the Improvement of Living and Working Conditions. *Shiftwork in the textile industry: case studies of* *innovations: Belgium.* Dublin: The Foundation, 1982.

298. European Foundation for the Improvement of Living and Working conditions. *Wage payment systems, surveys: Belgium.* Dublin: The Foundation, 1982.

299. Industrial Relations Services. "Belgium: coping with the recession." *European Industrial Relations Review,* 100 (May 1982), 10-12.

300. Industrial Relations Services. "Belgium: industrial action and the law." *European Industrial Relations Review,* 104 (September 1982), 12-13.

301. Industrial Relations Services. "Belgium: legislating on privacy." *European Industrial Relations Review,* 106 (November 1982), 15-16.

302. Industrial Relations Services. "Belgium: pay indexation reformed." *European Industrial Relations Review,* 99 (April 1982), 19-20.

303. Van der Bulcke, D. and Halsberghe, E. *Effets des entreprises multinationales sur l'emploi: étude du cas de la Belgique.* Geneva: I.L.O., 1982. iii, 70p.

304. European Centre for Work and Society. *Growing up without work: two case studies.* Assen: Vangarum, 1983. 99p.

305. Industrial Relations Services. "Belgium: new approaches to personal leave." *European Industrial Relations Review,* 117 (October 1983), 23-4.

306. Willard, J. C. "France en position mediane pour les couts salariaux." *Economie et Statistique,* 156 (June 1983), 25-41.

307. Blanpain, R. "Recent trends in collective bargaining in Belgium." *International Labour Review,* 123, 3 (May-June 1984), 319-32.

308. Industrial Relations Services. "Belgium: new technology agreement." *European Industrial Relations Review,* 121 (February 1984), 17-19.

309. Industrial Relations Services. "Belgium: recruitment agreement." *European Industrial Relations Review,* 122 (March 1984), 16-19.

310. Industrial Relations Services. "Belgium: working time experiments." *European Industrial Relations Review* 120 (January 1984), 7-8.

See also 17, 113, 156.

Belize

311. Ashcraft, N. "Economic opportunities and patterns of work: the case of British Honduras." *Human Organisation*, 31, 4 (Winter 1972), 425-33.

312. Henry, Z. *Labour relations and industrial conflict in Commonwealth Caribbean countries.* Port-of-Spain: Columbus Publishers, 1972. xii, 283p.

313. International Labour Organisation. *Belize: establishment of social security scheme: project findings and recommendations.* Geneva: I.L.O., 1981. vii, 88p.

Bolivia

314. United States. Bureau of Labour Statistics. *Labor law and practice in Bolivia.* Washington: U.S.G.P.O., 1966.

315. Magill, John. *Labour unions and political socialization: a case study of Bolivian workers.* New York: Praeger, 1974.

316. Lora, Guillermo. *A history of the Bolivian labour movement.* Cambridge: Cambridge University Press, 1977. 408p.

317. National Union of Mineworkers (U.K.) *Trade union and human rights in Chile and Bolivia.* London: N.U.M., 1977.

318. Nash, June. *We eat the mines and the mines eat us.* New York: Columbia University Press, 1979. 363p.

319. National Union of Mineworkers (U.K.) *Bolivia: report of a NUM delegation in July 1979.* London: N.U.M., 1979.

Botswana

320. United States. Bureau of Labor Statistics. *Labor law and practice in Botswana.* Washington: U.S.G.P.O., 1968.

321. Hartland-Thunberg, Penelope. *Botswana: an African growth economy.* Westview Press, 1979.

322. Bell, Morag. "Rural-urban movement among Botswana's skilled manpower." *Africa*, 50, 4 (1980), 404-21.

323. Gunn, Andrew. "Botswana's brigades: the thorny road to self-sufficiency." *Friends Quarterly*, 22 (April 1980), 258-65.

324. Moyo, Nelson. "The application of incomes policy in the private sector, with reference to the strike of bank employees in 1974." Harvey, C. (ed.) *Papers on the economy of Botswana.* London: Heinemann, 1981. p.196-208.

325. Weedon, Ray and Ystgaard, Odd. "Railways, immigrants, mining and cattle: problems of measurement in Botswana's national income accounts." Harvey, C. (ed.) *Papers on the economy of Botswana.* London: Heinemann, 1981. p.220-51.

See also 32, 50, 58, 144.

Brazil

326. Sallas, G. A. *Labor law and practice in Brazil.* Washington: U.S.G.P.O., 1967.

327. Rosenbaum, Harris Jon and Tyler, William G. (eds.) *Contemporary Brazil: issues in economic and political development.* New York: Praeger, 1972.

328. Erickson, K. P. *The Brazilian corporative state and working class politics.* Berkeley: University of California Press, 1977.

329. Schlagheck, James L. *The political, economic and labour climate in Brazil.* University of Pennsylvania, Wharton School, Industrial Research Unit, 1977.

330. Tolosa, H. C. "Causes of urban poverty in Brazil." *World Development,* 6 (September-October 1978), 1087-1101.

331. Fonseca, Claudia. "Education for rural development in Brazil." *Community Development Journal,* 14 (April 1979), 98-105.

332. Oakley, P. "Participation in development in North-East Brazil." *Community Development Journal,* 15 (January 1980), 10-22.

333. Levine, R. M. *Urban workers under the Brazilian Republic, 1889-1937.* Glasgow: Glasgow University, Institute of Latin American Studies, 1981.

334. Rossi, José W. "Income distribution in Brazil: a regional approach." *Journal of Development Studies,* 17 (January 1981), 226-34.

335. Humphrey, John. *Capitalist control and workers' struggle in the Brazilian auto industry.* Princeton University Press, 1982.

336. Jallade, Jean-Pierre. "Basic education and income inequality in

Brazil." *World Development*, 10 (March 1982), 187-97.

337. Morley, S. A. *Labor markets and inequitable growth: the case of authoritarian capitalism in Brazil.* Cambridge: Cambridge University Press, 1982.

338. Tyler, Christina. "Trade unionism in Brazil." *Third World Quarterly*, 4 (April 1982), 312-20.

339. Humphrey, J. "The growth of female employment in Brazilian manufacturing industry in the 1970s." *Journal of Development Studies*, 20 (July 1984), 224-47.

340. Sussekind, A. "The influence of international labour standards in Brazilian legislation." *International Labour Review*, 123, 4 (July-August 1984), 441-56.

See also 2, 4.

Bulgaria

341. Michev, D. and Kalaora, B. *Georgi Dimitrov and the trade union movement.* Sofia: Sofia Press, 1976. 269p.

342. Hadjinikolov, V., Mladenov, D., Issoussov, M. and Vedikov, S. *History of the Bulgarian trade unions.* Sofia: Sofia Press, 1977. 303p.

343. Beyazov, T., Bozhilov, Y., Avramov, T. and Blitznakov, Y. *Employment pattern and manpower change in the People's Republic of Bulgaria.* Geneva: I.L.O., 1980.

344. Detchev, K. *Participation of the working people in the management of enterprises in the People's Republic of Bulgaria.* Geneva: I.L.O., 1980. 8p.

345. Zhivkov, T. *New conception of labour and labour relations in socialist Bulgaria.* Sofia: Sofia Press, 1983.

346. Thirkell, John. "Brigade organisation and industrial relations strategy in Bulgaria 1978-83." *Industrial Relations Journal*, 16, 1 (Spring 1985), 33-43.

Burma

347. International Labour Organisation. *The trade union situation in Burma.* Geneva: I.L.O., 1962. 74p.

348. Norwood, Janet L. *Labor law and practice in the Union of Burma.* Washington: U.S.G.P.O., 1964. 59p.

Cameroon

349. Warmington, W. A. *A West African trade union: a case study of the Cameroon Development Corporation Workers' Union and its relations with the employers.* Oxford: Oxford University Press, 1960. 150p.

350. Nouga, Adalbert. *Les programmes d'emploi dans les pays en voie de développement: l'exemple de Cameroun.* Fribourg: Editions Universitaires Fribourg, 1980. 80p.

351. Cameroun. *Guide permanent du travail at de l'emploi au Cameroun.* Le Vesinet: Ediena, 1982.

Loose-leaf reference book.

352. International Labour Organisation. *République uniédé Cameroun: développement et institutionalisation de l'education ouvrière.* Geneva: I.L.O., 1982. 15p.

353. Hodsdon, D. F. "Problems of rural workers' organisation: the Camerounian experience." *International Labour Review,* 122, 6 (November-December 1983), 747-59.

354. Leunde, E. *Legislation Camerounaise du travail.* Yaounde: Editions C.L.E., 1983. v, 89p.

See also 28, 148.

Canada

355. *Relations Industrielles/Industrial Relations.* Quarterly journal in English and French on Canadian industrial relations published by Departement des Relations Industrielles, Université Laval, 1946-.

356. Logan, H. A. *Trade unions in Canada: their development and functioning.* Toronto: Macmillan, 1948. 639p.

357. McGill University. Industrial Relations Centre, Annual Conference. *Reports.* Montreal, 1948-.

358. Jamieson, Stuart. *Times of trouble: labour unrest and industrial conflict in Canada, 1900-66.* Ottawa: Privy Counci Office, 1968. (Task Force on Labour Relations study 22).

359. Task Force on Labour Relations. *Canadian industrial relations.* Ottawa: Privy Council Office, 1968. 250p.

360. Wood, W. D. and Kumar, Pradeep. *The current industrial* *relations scene in Canada.* Annual. Queen's University at Kingston, Industrial Relations Centre, 1973-.

361. Woods, H. D. *Labour policy in Canada.* Second edition. Toronto: Macmillan, 1973. 377p.

362. Bain, George Sayers. *Union growth and public policy in Canada.* Canada Department of Labour, Employment Relations Branch, 1978. 47p.

363. Jamieson, Stuart. *Industrial conflict in Canada 1966-75.* Economic Council of Canada, 1979. 70p. (Discussion paper 142).

364. Kumar, Pradeep. *Canadian industrial relations information, sources, technical notes and glossary.* Queen's University at Kingston, Industrial Relations Centre, 1979. 166p.

365. Pentland, H. Clare. "The Canadian industrial relations system: some formative factors." *Labour/Le Travailleur,* 4, 4 (1979), 9-23.

366. Weiler, Paul. *Reconcilable differences: new directions in Canadian labour law.* Toronto: Carswell, 1980. 335p.

367. Arthurs, H. W., Carter, D. D. and Glasbeek, H. J. *Labour law and industrial relations in Canada.* Deventer: Kluwer, 1981. 291p.

368. Reasons, Charles E., Ross, Lois L. and Paterson, Craig. *Assault on the worker: occupational health and safety in Canada.* Toronto: Butterworth, 1981. 312p.

369. Task Force on Labour Market Development. *Labour market development in the 1980s.* Employment and Immigration Canada, 1981. 243p.

370. Woods, H. D. and Goldenberg, Shirley B. "Industrial relations research in Canada." Doeringer, Peter, (ed.) *Industrial relations in international perspective: Essays on research and policy.* New York: Holmes & Meier, 1981. p.22-75.

371. Anderson, John C. and Gunderson, Morley (eds.) *Union-management relations in Canada.* Don Mills, Ontario: Addison-Wesley, 1982. 584p.

372. Boivin, Jean and Guilbault, Jacques. *Les relations patronales-syndicales au Quebec.* Quebec: Chicoutimi, 1982. 309p.

373. Briskin, Linda and Yanz, Lynda (eds.) *Union sisters: women in the labour movement.* Toronto: The Women's Press, 1983.

374. Craig, Alton W. J. *The system of industrial relations in Canada.* Scarborough, Ontario: Prentice-Hall, 1983. 408p.

375. Finkelman, Jacob and Goldenberg, Shirley B. *Collective bargaining in the public service: the federal experience in Canada.* Canada: Institute for Research on Public Policy, 1983. Two volumes.

376. Palmer, Bryan D. *Working-class experience: the rise and reconstitution of Canadian labour, 1800-1980.* Toronto: Butterworth, 1983. 347p.

377. Phillips, Paul and Phillips, Erin. *Women and work inequality in the labour market.* Toronto: James Lorimer, 1983. 205p.

378. Labour Canada. *Directory of labour organizations in Canada.* Annual. Ottawa: Ministry of Supply and Services.

379. Labour Canada. *Strikes and lockouts in Canada.* Annual. Ottawa: Ministry of Supply and Services.

380. Labour Canada. *Industrial relations research in Canada.* Biennial. Ottawa: Ministry of Supply and Services.

381. *Labour/Le Travail.* Journal of Canadian labour studies. St. Johns, Newfoundland: Memorial University of Newfoundland, Department of History, Biannual.

382. Lowe, Graham S. and Krahn, Harvey J. (eds.) *Working Canadians: readings in the sociology of work, and industry.* Toronto: Methuen, 1984. 380p.

383. Thompson, Mark and Swimmer, Gene (eds.) *Conflict or compromise: the future of public sector industrial relations.* Montreal: The Institute for Research on Public Policy, 1984. 476p.

384. Université Laval. *Congrès des relations industrielles de l'Université Laval.* Quebec: Les Presses de l'Université Laval, Annual.

See also 61.

Chad

385. Danaho, R. *Perspectives d'emploi et les besoins en personnel qualifié au cours de la decennie 1971-1980: travaux préparatoires pour le plan annexe pour l'emploi et la formation professionelle (1971-1980).* Fort Lany: Chad, Direction du Plan et du Developpement, 1972. vi, 120p.

386. Danaho, R. *Perspectives de la production, de la productivité et de l'emploi dans le secteur moderne et éléments pour une politique de l'emploi au cours de la période 1971-1980.* Fort Lany: Chad, Direction du Plan et du Developpement, 1972. vii, 102p.

387. Danaho, R. *Emploi et le sous emploi dans le secteur agricole et en zone rurale: situation en 1970.* Fort Lany: Chad, Direction du Plan et du Developpement, 1973. xiii, 156p.

Chile

388. Morris, James O. *Elites, intellectuals and consensus: a study of the social question and industrial relations in Chile.* New York State School of Industrial And Labor Relations, 1966.

389. Gregory, Peter. *Industrial wages in Chile.* New York State School of Industrial and Labor Relations, 1967.

390. Angell, Alan. *Politics and the labour market in Chile.* Oxford: Oxford University Press, 1972.

391. Seton, Francis. *Shadow wages in the Chilean economy.* Paris: O.E.C.D., 1972.

392. Raptis, M. *Revolution and counter-revolution in Chile: a dossier on workers' participation in the revolutionary process.* New York: Allison & Busby, 1974.

393. International Labour Organisation. *The trade union situation in Chile.* Geneva: I.L.O., 1975.

394. Stallings, Barbara. *Class conflict and economic development in Chile, 1958-1973.* Stanford University Press, 1978.

395. Roddick, Jaqueline and Haworth, Nigel. *Chile 1924 and 1979: labour policy and industrial relations through two revolutions.* Glasgow: University of Glasgow, Institute of Latin American Studies, 1984. 34p.

See also 2, 4.

China

396. Hook, B. G. "Some aspects of social and cultural change in contemporary China." *Royal Society of Arts Journal,* 126 (October 1978), 669-77.

397. Klatt, W. "China's food and fuel under new management." *International Affairs*, 54 (January 1978), 60-74.

398. Nolan, Peter. "Inequality of income between town and countryside in the People's Republic of China in the mid-1950s." *World Development*, 7 (April-May 1979), 447-65.

399. Rawski, T. G. "Economic growth and employment in China." *World Development*, 7 (August-September 1979), 767-82.

400. Young, Michael. "China's co-op shop." *New Society* (1st November 1979), 241-2.

401. Braddick, B. and Foy, N. "Management after Mao." *Management Today* (August 1980), 46-9.

402. Henley, John S. and Chen, P. "A note on the appearance, disappearance and reappearance of dual functioning trade unions in the People's Republic of China." *British Journal of Industrial Relations*, 19, 1 (March 1981), 87-93.

403. Griffin, K. and Smith, A. "The pattern of income inequality in rural China." *Oxford Economic Papers*, 34 (March 1982), 172-206.

404. White, G. "Urban unemployment and labour allocation policies in post-Mao China." *World Development*, 10 (August 1982), 613-32.

405. "The All-China Federation of Trade Unions in the Cultural Revolution." *Australian Journal of Politics and History*, 29, 1 (1983), 50-62.

Christmas Island

406. Waters, Les. *The Union of Christmas Island Workers.* London: Allen & Unwin, 1983.

Colombia

407. Braun, Kurt. *Labor law and practice in Colombia.* Washington: U.S.G.P.O., 1962.

408. Zschock, D. K. *Manpower perspective of Colombia.* Princeton University, Industrial Relations Section, 1967.

409. International Labour Organisation. *Towards full employment: a programme for Colombia.* Geneva: I.L.O., 1970.

410. Urrutia, Miguel. *The development of the Colombian labor* *movement.* Yale University Press, 1970.

411. Agosin, Manuel R. "Development patterns and labour absorption in Colombian manufacturing." *Journal of Development Studies,* 12 (July 1976), 351-63.

412. Huddle, D.L. "An analysis of the saving behaviour of a group of Colombian artisan entrepreneurs." *World Development,* 7 (August-September 1979), 847-64.

413. Thirsk, W. R. "Aggregation bias and the sensibility of income distribution to change in the composition of demand: the case of Colombia." *Journal of Development Studies,* 16 (October 1979), 50-66.

414. Twinam, Ann. *Miners, merchants and farmers in colonial Colombia.* University of Texas Press, 1982.

415. Ridler, N. "Labour force and land distributional effects of agricultural technology: a case study of coffee." *World Development,* 11 (July 1983), 593-9.

Congo

416. International Labour Organisation. Expanded Programme of Technical Assistance. *Rapport au Gouvernement du Congo sur la formation et le perfectionnement du personnel des cadres subalternes et moyens.* Geneva: I.L.O., 1962. Various paginations.

417. International Labour Organisation. *Congo: rapport de la Mission ... sur le marché de l'emploi et les services chargés des problèmes de l'emploi.* Geneva: I.L.O., 1981.

418. International Labour Organisation. Jobs and Skills Programme for Africa. *Secteur informal et emploi en République du Congo.* Addis Ababa: I.L.O., 1982. 52p.

See also 109.

Costa Rica

419. Lom, H. and Lizanoff, E. "National Wages Board and minimum wage policy in Costa Rica." *Pakistan Labour Gazette,* 38 (October-December 1977), 13-21.

420. Lizano, Fait E. "Towards a national employment policy: the case of Costa Rica." *International Labour Review,* 120, 3 (May-June 1981),

361-74.

421. Alexander, M. "Surviving in a Latin American democracy." *Swiss Review of World Affairs*, 33, 6 (September 1983), 8-10.

Includes material on unemployment.

Cuba

422. Zeitlin, Maurice. *Revolutionary politics and the Cuban working class.* Princeton: Princeton University Press, 1967. 306p.

423. Mesa-Lago, Carmela. *The labour sector and socialist distribution in Cuba.* New York: Praeger, 1968. 250p.

424. Bengelsdorf, C. and Hageman, A. "Emerging from underdevelopment: women and work in Cuba." *Race and Class*, 19, 4 (Spring 1978), 361-78.

425. Pollitt, B. H. *Agrarian reform and the "agricultural proletariat" in Cuba, 1958-66: some notes.* Glasgow: Glasgow University, Institute of Latin American Studies, 1979. 33p.

426. MacEwan, A. *Revolution and economic development in Cuba.* New York: St. Martin's Press, 1981. xvi, 265p.

427. Roca, S. "Economic policy and institutional change in socialist Cuba." *Journal of Economic Issues*, 17 (June 1983), 405-13.

Includes material on the labour market.

Cyprus

428. House, W. J. "Labour market segmentation: evidence from Cyprus." *World Development*, 12 (April 1984), 403-18.

Czechoslovakia

429. International Labour Organisation. Committee on Freedom of Association. *Trade union rights in Czechoslovakia.* London: Staples Press for the I.L.O., 1953. 45p.

430. Revolutionary Trade Union Movement. *Trade unions in Czechoslovakia.* Prague: The Movement, 1973. 86p.

431. *Trade unions and democracy.* Prague: Prace, 1978. 123p.

432. Fisera, F. *Workers' councils in Czechoslovakia, 1968-9: documents and essays.* New York: St. Martin's Press, 1979. 200p.

433. Navratil, O. and Pudik, V. *Czechoslovak trade unions and the labour law.* Prague: Prace, 1979. 83p.

434. Dolejsi, B. "Labour productivity, wages and the satisfaction of the needs of the population." *Eastern European Economics*, 19, 1 (Fall 1980), 77-100.

435. Czechoslovak Research Institute of Labour and Social Affairs. *Bibliography, 1965-1980.* Bratislava: The Institute, 1981. 71p.

436. Fremr, J. "Evolution des salaires des travailleurs en République Socialiste Tchechoslovaque selon les branches, période 1976-1980." *Demosta*, 14, 3 (1981), 85-9.

See also 69, 74, 88, 123.

Denmark

437. Galenson, Walter. *The Danish system of labor relations: a study in industrial peace.* New York: Russell & Russell, 1969. 321p.

438. Blum, A. A. "Who belongs to unions in Denmark?" *Industrial Relations Journal,* 3, 3 (Autumn 1972), 49-59.

439. United States. Bureau of Labor Statistics. *Labor law and practice in Denmark.* Washington: U.S.G.P.O., 1972. viii, 71p.

440. Landsorganisationen i Danmark. *Co-ownership and co-determination: the Danish government bills on economic and industrial democracy.* Copenhagen: L.O., 1973. 26p.

441. Blum, A. A. and Ponak, A. "White collar unions in Denmark." *Relations Industrielles,* 29, 1 (1974), 65-82.

442. Bunnage, David, Mortensen, Nils and Rosdahl, Anders. *Technology and the worker: the consequences of technology for work and qualification levels within three industries.* Copenhagen: Kommission hos Teknisk Forlag, 1974. 251p.

443. Denmark. Arbejdsmiljogruppen af 1972. *Work environment, meaningful jobs, ejection from the labour market.* Copenhagen: Statens Trykningskenter, 1974.110p.

444. Kuhlmann, S. *Danish labour market conditions, 1974.* Copenhagen: Ministry of Labour, Economic-Statistic Adviser, 1974. 380p.

445. Organisation for Economic Co-operation and Development. *Manpower policy in Denmark.* Paris: O.E.C.D., 1974. 59p.

446. Bunnage, David and Rosdahl, Anders. *Technology and the worker: attitudes of workers to the work situation, job change and training.* Copenhagen: Kommission hos Teknisk Forlag, 1976. 197p.

447. Gundelach, Peter and Redder, K. W. *The scope of labour mobility.* Copenhagen: Kommission hos Teknisk Forlag, 1976. 109p.

448. Haargaard, Jytte, Jensen, Kirsten, Just, Nielsen, Birthe and Redder, K. W. *The consequences of mobility.* Copenhagen: Kommission hos Teknisk Forlag, 1976.

449. Hillestrom, Karsten. *The mobility process.* Copenhagen: Kommission hos Teknisk Forlag, 1976. 115p.

450. Dylander, B. "Working life research in Denmark." *Economic and*

Industrial Democracy, 1, 2 (May 1980), 171-95.

451. European Foundation for the Improvement of Living and Working Conditions. *Institutionalised forms of participation in Danish companies.* Dublin: The Foundation, 1980.

452. European Foundation for the Improvement of Living and Working Conditions. *Safety and health at the workplace: Denmark.* Dublin: The Foundation, 1980.

453. Mire. J. *Country labour profile: Denmark.* Washington: U.S.G.P.O., 1980. 8p.

454. Dekov, E., Nielsen, L., Roos, P. and Toft, A. *Workers' participation in decisions within undertakings in Denmark.* Geneva: I.L.O., 1981. 7p.

455. Denmark. Arbejdsministeriet. *Labour market and labour market policy, May 1981.* Copenhagen: Arbejdsministeriet, 1981. 87p.

456. European Foundation for the Improvement of Living and Working Conditions. *Shiftwork in the chemical industry: surveys: Denmark.* Dublin: The Foundation, 1981.

457. European Foundation for the Improvement of Living and Working Conditions. *Institutionalised forms of participation in companies.* Dublin: The Foundation, 1981.

458. European Foundation for the Improvement of Living and Working Conditions. *Shiftwork in the services sector: Denmark.* Dublin: The Foundation, 1981.

459. Industrial Relations Services. "Denmark: new industrial relations ground-rules." *European Industrial Relations Review*, 86 (March 1981), 6-9.

460. Lindegaard, P. *Conciliation system in Denmark.* Geneva: I.L.O., 1981. 3p.

461. Tronsgaard, H. *Analysis of Danish sex-linked attitude: toward married women's employment, forms of childcare and the preferred occupational status.* Copenhagen: Teknisk Forlag, 1981. 173p.

462. Dansk Sygeplejerad. *E.O.P. handbook for nurses.* Copenhagen: D.S., 1982. 126p.

463. European Foundation for the Improvement of Living and Working Conditions. *Shiftwork in the health services: case studies of innovations: Denmark.* Dublin: The Foundation, 1982.

464. European Foundation for the Improvement of Living and Working Conditions. *Wage payment systems: surveys: Denmark.* Dublin: The Foundation, 1982.

465. Industrial Relations Services. "Denmark: new low pay report." *European Industrial Relations Review,* 102 (July 1982), 20-1.

466. Industrial Relations Services. "Denmark: proposed closed shop legislation." *European Industrial Relations Review,* 98 (March 1982), 18-19.

467. Boelsgaard, K. *Trade union movement in Denmark.* Copenhagen: Ministry of Foreign Affairs, 1983. 4p.

468. Bruun, I., Konner, M. and Koefoed, E. *Dossier on interaction between the labour market and the educational system in Denmark.* Berlin: European Centre for the Development of Vocational Training, 1983. 35p.

469. European Foundation for the Improvement of Living and Working Conditions. *Survey of research on working time and leisure time: Denmark.* Dublin: The Foundation, 1983.

470. Industrial Relations Services. "Denmark: central pay framework." *European Industrial Relations Review,* 111 (April 1983), 20-2.

471. Industrial Relations Services. "Denmark: union launch investment fund company," *European Industrial Relations Review,* 116 (September 1983), 6-7.

472. Gill, Colin. "Industrial relations in Denmark." *Industrial Relations Journal,* (Spring 1984), 46-57.

See also 121, 154, 156.

Ecuador

473. Brackett, Joseph A. *Labor law and practice in Ecuador.* Washington: U.S.G.P.O., 1963.

Egypt

474. International Institute for Labour Studies. *Regional seminar on problems of planning the labour force and it employment.* Cairo: Institute of National Planning, 1963.

475. Handy, M. *Manpower requirements for the U.A.R. for the period 1960-1985.* Cairo: Institute of National Planning, 1964. vi 127p.

476. Clarke, Joan. *Labour law and practice in the United Arab Republic (Egypt).* Washington: U.S.G.P.O., 1965. 99p.

477. Kamel. M. *Monograph on the settlement of labour disputes in the U.A.R.* Cairo: [?], 1968. 196p.

478. Organisation for Economic Co-operation and Development. *[Proceedings of the] Seminar on Manpower Planning, 1968, Cairo.* Cairo: Institute of National Planning, 1968. Various paginations.

479. Mongi, M. and Hanafi, M. *Labour absorption in the Egyptian economy.* Cairo: Institute of National Planning, 1970.

480. Nagi, M. H. *Labour force and employment in Egypt: a demographic and socioeconomic analysis.* New York: Praeger, 1971. xviii, 285p.

481. Vaidyanathan, K. E. *Seminar on demographic factors in manpower planning in Arab countries: the household sample survey as a tool for manpower analysis: a case study of lower Egypt.* Geneva: International Institute for Labour Studies, 1971. 13p.

482. Nagi, M. H. "Child labor in rural Egypt." *Rural Sociology,* 37, 4 (December 1972), 623-7.

483. Shahat, M. A. and Nassar, S. Z. "Estimates of labour surplus in agriculture in Egypt." *Egypte Contemporaine,* 65, 355 (January 1974), 85-93.

484. Blahusiak, J. *Arab Republic of Egypt: manpower assessment and planning.* Geneva: I.L.O., 1974. 30p.

485. Eltarhu, E. "Egyptian trade union movement in a nutshell." *Labour,* 10 (June 1974), 37-44.

486. Choucri, N., Eckaus, R. S. and Mohie-eldine, A. *Migration and employment in the construction sector: critical factors in Egyptian development*. Cambridge, Mass.: Massachusets Institute of Technology. Technological Planning Programme, 1978. 167p.

487. Hammam, M. "Egypt's working women: textile workers of Chubra El-Kheima." *Merip Reports*, 82 (1979) 3-12.

488. McVoy, E. C. and Clarke, J. *Country labor profile: Egypt.* Washington: U.S.G.P.O., 1979. 8p.

489. Sayed, S. *Workers' participation in management: the Egyptian experience.* Cairo: American University in Cairo Press, 1978. xiii, 141p.

490. Abdel-Fadil, M. *Political economy of Nasserism: a study in employment and income distribution policies in urban Egypt, 1952-72.* Cambridge: Cambridge University Press, 1980. xii, 140p.

491. Guindy, W. A. *Participation of workers in decision-making in Egypt.* Geneva: I.L.O., 1981. 2p.

492. International Labour Organisation. *Employment opportunities and equity in a changing economy: Egypt in the 1980s: a labour market approach: draft report of a mission...* Geneva: I.L.O., 1981. viii, 245p.

493. Hansen, B. and Radwan, S. *Employment opportunities and equity in a changing economy: Egypt in the 1980s: a labour market approach.* Geneva: I.L.O., 1982. xviii, 292p.

494. Hansen, B. and Radwan, S. "Employment planning in Egypt: an insurance policy for the future." *International Labour Review*, 121, 5 (September-October 1982), 535-51.

495. International Labour Organisation. *Report of the National Tripartite Seminar on the development of labour relations in Egypt, Cairo, 1980.* Geneva: I.L.O., 1982. 8p.

496. Hodsdon, D. F. *Al-Nacabal'ana li'ummal alzira wal-ray bijamhowiyyat mist al'arabiyya.* Geneva: I.L.O., 1983. iii, 55p.

   Field study of agricultural workers and their unions. English translation available.

497. Hodsdon, D. F. *General trade union of workers in agriculture and irrigation: Arab Republic of Egypt.* Geneva: I.L.O., 1983. 37p.

See also 6, 141.

El Salvador

498. Kleiner, Karol C. and Sallas, Gustav A. *Labor law and practice in El Salvador.* Washington: U.S.G.P.O., 1964. 65p.

499. Dominguez Pena, J. M. *Los reursos humanos en el desarrollo industrial de El Salvador.* San Salvador: Universidad de El Salvador, Faculdad de Ciencias Economicas, 1971. x, 263p.

See also 42.

Equatorial Guinea

500. International Labour Organisation. *Guinea Ecuatorial: administracion del trabajo.* Geneva: I.L.O., 1982. 13p.

Ethiopia

501. Suter, Ann C. *Labor law and practice in the Empire of Ethiopia.* Washington: U.S.G.P.O., 1966.

502. Ginzberg, Eli. *Manpower strategy for developing countries: lessons from Ethiopia.* Columbia University Press, 1967.

503. Wilkin, D. "Refugees and British administration policy in North Kenya 1936-1938. *African Affairs,* 79 (October 1980), 510-30.

Ethiopian refugees.

Finland

504. Elvander, N. "Collective bargaining and incomes policy in the Nordic countries: a comparative analysis." *British Journal of Industrial Relations*, 11, 2 (July 1974), 417-37.

505. Lilja, K. and Tainio, R. *Sociological research in the area of working life in Finland.* [?]: [?]. 1976.

506. Berglind, H., Hanisch, T. and Haavio-Mannila, E. (eds.) *Sociology of work in the Nordic countries: themes and perspectives.* Scandinavian Sociological Association, 1978.

507. Matheson, D. K. "Ideology, political action and the Finnish working class." *Commentationes Scientiarum Socialum,* (October 1979).

508. Oivio, P. and Somerto, P. "What about the workers?" *Euromoney,* (May 1980), 16-17.

509. Koskimies, J. "Finland." Blum, A. A. (ed.) *International handbook of industrial relations.* London: Aldwych Press, 1981.

510. Tyrvcinen, T. "The economic background of strikes in Finland." *Bank of Finland Monthly Bulletin,* 55, 10 (1981) 24-8.

511. Addison, J. T. "Finnish incomes policy: unions and other constraints." *Journal of Labour Research,* 3 (Summer 1982), 335-48.

512. Lilja, K. *Workers' workplace organisations: their conceptual identification , historically specific conditions and manifestations.* Helsinki: Helsinki School of Economics, 1983. 227p.

See also 80, 154.

France

513. Saposs, D. *The labor movement in post war France.* New York: Russell & Russell, 1972.

First published 1931.

514. Seyfarth, Shaw, Fairweather and Geraldson. *Labor relations and the law in France and the United States: a comparative study.* University of Michigan, 1972.

515. Organisation for Economic Co-operation and development. *Manpower policy in France.* Paris: O.E.C.D., 1973.

516. Shorter, E. and Tilly, C. *Strikes in France, 1830-1968.*

Cambridge: Cambridge University Press, 1974.

517. Weiss, Dimitri. "Information économique, entreprise et relations collectives: un dossier français." *Relations Industrielles*, 29, 1 (1974), 3-64.

518. Mallet, Serge (ed.) *Essays on the new working class.* Telos Press, 1975.

519. Mallet, Serge. *The new working class.* Nottingham: Spokesman, 1975.

520. Badie, Bertrand. *Strategie de la grève.* Paris: Fondation National des Sciences Politiques, 1976.

521. Moss, Bernard H. *The origins of the French labour movement, 1830-1914.* Berkeley: University of California Press, 1976.

522. Kassalow, Everett M. "Christian trade unionism in France: a left socialist experience." *Relations Industrielles*, 32, 1 (1977), 3-17.

523. Pelletier, Robert. "Accounting to employees, French fashion." *Personnel Management*, 9, 9 (September 1977), 29-31, 39.

524. Smith, W. Rand. "Attitudes towards workers' control in France." *Socialist Review*, 25 (November 1977), 877-85.

525. Gallie, Duncan. *In search of the new working class.* Cambridge: Cambridge University Press, 1978.

526. Jenny, Frederic. "Wage rates, concentration and unionization in French manufacturing industry." *Journal of Industrial Economics*, 26 (June 1978), 315-27.

527. Lavau, Georges. "The changing relations between trade unions and working class parties in France." *Government and Opposition*, 13 (Autumn 1978), 437-57.

528. Sellier, François. "L'appreciation des politiques du DGB par les syndicats francais." *Relations Industrielles*, 33 3 (1978), 606-17.

529. Dubois, Pierre. *Sabotage in industry.* Harmondsworth: Penguin, 1979.

530. Granotier, Bernard. *Les travailleurs immigrés en France.* Paris: Maspero, 1979.

531. Kennedy-Brenner, Carliene. *Foreign workers and immigration policy: the case of France.* Paris: O.E.C.D., 1979.

532. Slack, Edward. "Plant-level bargaining in France." *Industrial Relations Journal*, 11, 4 (September-October 1980), 27-38.

533. Weiss, Dimitri. *Relations industrielles*. Second edition. Paris: Sirez, 1980.

534. Rose, M. "Mitterand, militants and superboss: industrial relations in France's socialist experiment." *Personnel Management*, 13, 9 (September 1981), 31-5.

535. Bornstein, Sam and Richardson, Al. *Two steps back: communists and the wider labour movement 1939-45*. Ilford: Socialist Platform, 1982.

536. DeAngelis, R. A. *Blue collar workers and politics: a French paradox*. London: Croom Helm, 1982.

537. Ross George. *Workers and communists in France*. University of Columbia Press, 1982.

538. Caire, Guy. "Procedures de réglement pacifique des conflits collectifs en France." *Relations Industrielles*, 38, 1 (1983), 3-25.

539. Eyraud, F. "Principles of union action in the engineering industries of Great Britain and France." *British Journal of Industrial Relations*, 21, 3 (November 1983), 358-76.

540. Caire, Guy. "Recent trends in collective bargaining in France." *International Labour Review*, 123, 6 (November-December 1984), 723-42.

541. Smith, W. Rand. "Dynamics of plural unionism in France: the CGT, CFDT and industrial conflict." *British Journal of Industrial Relations*, 22, 1 (March 1984), 15-33.

See also 14, 40, 52, 59, 76, 78, 113, 127, 132, 136, 140, 156, 157.

Gabon

542. Lefebvre, F. J. "Organisation du travail au Gabon." *Cooperation Technique*, 75 (December 1974), 41-5.

543. Mariers, G. R. *République Gabonaise: étude de l'emploi, des salaires et des prix.* Lome: Regional Economic Research and Documentation Centre, 1974. 28p.

544. Gabon. Ministère du Travail et de l'Emploi. *Situation de l'emploi au Gabon de 1977 a 1981.* Libreville: La Ministère, 1981. 14p.

Includes statistical tables.

545. Sobotchou, J. P. "Modes normaux de dissolution du contrat de travail a durée indeterminée au Gabon." *Penant*, 92, 776 (April-June 1982), 9-40.

Gambia

546. Gambia. Central Statistics Division. *Urban labour force survey 1974/75.* Bathurst: The Division, 1975.

547. Peil, M. "West African urban craftsmen." *Journal of Developing Areas*, 14, 1(October 1979), 3-22.

See also 12, 79, 148.

Germany, East

548. United States. Bureau of Labor Statistics. *Labor law and practice in East Germany.* Washington: U.S.G.P.O., 1966. 48p.

549. Lederig, W. "Demographische Aspekte der Arbeitskraefterentwicklung in der DDR." *Sozialistische Arbeitswissenschaft*, 19, 1 (1975), 53-9.

550. Rehtanz, H. "Organisation of occupational safety in the German Democratic Republic." *International Labour Review*, 112, 6 (December 1975), 419-29.

551. Sachse, E. "Manpower planning and higher education in the German Democratic Republic." *International Labour Review*, 113, 3 (May-June 1976), 377-89.

552. Adler, F. "Work and personality development in the German Democratic Republic." *International Social Science Journal*, 32, 3

(1980), 443-63.

553. Herzog, Marianne. *From hand to mouth: women and piecework.* Harmondsworth: Penguin, 1980. 154p.

554. Pawloff, M. "Industrieroboter als Wirkungsrichtung des Wissenschaftlich-Technischen Fortschritts und Erleichterung der Menschlichen Arbeit." *Sozialistische Arbeitswissenschaft,* 1 (1981), 33-8.

English abstract available.

555. Bley, H., Freyer, H. and Mader, E. *Arbeitsoekonomie: Lehrbuch.* Berlin: Verlag die Wirtschaft, 1982. 720p.

Includes a 12-page bibliography.

556. Freier Deutscher Gewerkschaftsbund. *Geschichte des Freier Deutscher Gewerkschaftsbund.* Berlin: Verlag Tribuene, 1982. 831p.

See also 5, 69, 74, 88, 123.

Germany, West

557. Kirkwood, Thomas and Mewes, Horst. "The limits of trade union power in the capitalist order: the case of West German labour's quest for co-determination." *British Journal of Industrial Relations,* 14, 3 (November 1976), 295-305.

558. Keller, Berndt. "Public sector labor relations in West Germany." *Industrial Relations,* 17, 1 (February 1978), 18-31.

559. Miller, Doug. "Trade union workplace representation in the Federal Republic of Germany: an analysis of the post war Vertrauensleute policy of the German metalworkers' union 1952-77." *British Journal of Industrial Relations,* 16, 3 (November 1978), 335-54.

560. von Beyme, Klaus. "The changing relations between trade unions and the Social Democratic Party in West Germany." *Government and Opposition,* 13, 4 (October 1978), 399-415.

561. Clark, Jon. "Concerted action in the Federal Republic of Germany." *British Journal of Industrial Relations,* 17, 2 (July 1979), 242-58.

562. Hartmann, Heinz. "Works councils and the Iron Law of Oligarchy." *British Journal of Industrial Relations,* 17, 1 (March 1979), 70-82.

563. Hetzler, H. and Schienstock, G. "Federal Republic of Germany."

Roberts, B. C. (ed.) *Towards industrial democracy*. London: Croom Helm, 1979. p. 23-51.

564. Lawrence, Peter. *Managers and management in West Germany*. London: Croom Helm, 1980. 159p.

565. Leminsky, Gerhard. "Worker participation: the German experience." Martin, Benjamin and Kassalow, Everett (eds.) *Labour relations in advanced industrial societies: issues and problems*. Washington/New York: Carnegie Endowment, 1980. p. 139-60.

566. Keller, Berndt. "Determinants of the wage rate in the public sector." *British Journal of Industrial Relations*, 19, 3 (November 1981), 345-60.

567. Lewis, Roy and Clark, Jon. "Trade unions, industrial relations and employment legislation in Germany, 1868-1933." Kahn-Freund, Otto (ed.) *Labour law and politics in the Weimar Republic*. Oxford: Blackwell, 1981.
p.19-36.

568. Müller-Jentsch, Walter. "Strikes and strike trends in West Germany, 1950-78." *Industrial Relations Journal*, 12, 4 (Winter 1981), 36-57.

569. Streeck, Wolfgang. "Qualitative demands and the neo-corporatist manageability of industrial relations." *British Journal of Industrial Relations*, 19, 2(July 1981), 149-69.

570. Miller, Doug. "Social partnership and the determinants of workplace independence in West Germany." *British Journal of Industrial Relations*, 20, 1 (March 1982), 44-66.

571. Bergmann, Joachim and Müller-Jentsch, Walter. "The Federal Republic of Germany: cooperative unionism and dual bargaining system challenged." Barkin, Solomon (ed.) *Worker militancy and its consequences*. Second edition. New York/Washington/ London: Praeger, 1983. p. 229-77.

572. Altmann, Norbert. "Company performance policies and the role of the works council." Shigeyoshi, Tokunaga and Bergmann, Joachim (eds.) *Industrial relations in transition: the cases of Japan and the Federal Republic of Germany*. Tokyo: University of Tokyo Press/Campus-Verlag, 1984. p. 255-80.

573. Bunn, Ronald. "Employers' associations in the Federal Republic of Germany." Windmuller, John and Gladstone, Alan. *Employers* *associations and industrial relations: a comparative study.* Oxford: Oxford University Press, 1984. p. 169-201.

574. Deutschmann, Christoph. "Labour market segmentation and industrial relations in the Federal Republic of Germany." Shigeyoshi, Tokunaga and Bergmann, Joachim (eds.) *Industrial relations in transition: the cases of Japan and the Federal Republic of Germany.* Tokyo: University of Tokyo Press/Campus-Verlag, 1984. p. 59-76.

575. Müller-Jentsch, Walter. "Labor conflicts and class arguments: interpretations of the labour conflicts of the 1970s and conjectures on the future of trade unions." Jacobi, Otto, Jessop, Bob, Kastendiek, Hans and Regini, Marino (eds.) *Technological change, rationalization and industrial relations.* London: Croom Helm, 1984. Chapter 11.

576. Streeck, Wolfgang. *Industrial relations in West Germany.* London: Heinemann, 1984. 178p.

577. Webber, Douglas and Nass, Gabriele. "Employment policy in West Germany." Richardson, Jeremy and Henning, Roger (eds.) *Unemployment: policy responses of Western democracies.* London: Sage, 1984. p. 167-91.

See also 5, 37, 40, 47, 52, 57, 76, 78, 79, 99, 121, 127, 132, 140, 157.

Ghana

578. Ghana. Development Planning Secretariat. Manpower Division. *High level and skilled manpower survey in Ghana, 1968, and assessment of manpower situation (1971).* Accra: The Division, 1971. 63p.

579. Addo, N. O. "Employment and labour supply on Ghana's cocoa farms in the pre- and post-Aliens Compliance Order era." *Economic Bulletin of Ghana,* 21, 4 (1972), 33-50.

580. International Labour Organisation and Ghana. Management Development and Productivity Institute. *Report on project, results, conclusions and recommendations.* Geneva: I.L.O., 1972. iii, 130p.

581. Iwuji, E. C. *Employment promotion problems in the economic and social development of Ghana.* Geneva: International Institute for Labour Studies, 1972. 62p.

582. Peil, Margaret. *The Ghanaian factory worker.* Cambridge: Cambridge University Press, 1972. 254p.

583. Roemer, M. *Neoclassical employment model applied to Ghanaian* *manufacturing.* Cambridge, Mass.: Harvard University, Center for International Affairs, 1972. 35p.

584. Rourke, B. E. and Sakyi-Gyinae, S. K. "Agricultural and urban wage rates in Ghana." *Economic Bulletin of Ghana,* 2, 1 (1972), 3-13.

585. Rourke, B. E. and Cbeng, F. A. "Seasonality in the employment of casual agricultural labour in Ghana." *Economic Bulletin of Ghana,* 3, 3 (1973), 3-13.

586. Williams, T. O. and Ntim, S. M. "Public employment centres as a source of data on unemployment in Ghana." *Economic Bulletin of Ghana,* 3, 1 (1973), 16-26.

587. Abban, J. B. "Evaluation of high level manpower surveys in Ghana." *Economic Bulletin of Ghana,* 4, 2 (1974), 18-35.

588. Addo, N. O. "Foreign African workers in Ghana." *International Labour Review,* 109, 1 (January 1974), 47-68.

589. Damachi, Ukandi Godwin. *The role of trade unions in the development process, with a case study of Ghana.* New York: Praeger, 1974. 175p.

590. Damachi, U. G. "Government, employers and workers in Ghana: a study of the mutual perception of roles." *British Journal of Industrial Relations,* 14, 1 (March 1976), 26-34.

591. Jeffries, Richard. *Class, power and ideology in Ghana: the railwaymen of Sekondi.* Cambridge: Cambridge University Press, 1978. 244p.

592. Harris, D. S. *Country labor profile: Ghana.* Washington: U.S.G.P.O., 1980. 6p.

593. Date-Bah, E. *Rural women, their activities and technology in Ghana: an overview.* Geneva: I.L.O., 1981. ii, 82p.

594. Greenstreet, M. *Females in the agricultural labour force and non-formal education for rural development in Ghana.* The Hague: Institute of Social Studies, 1981. 22p.

595. International Labour Organisation. *Workers' participation in decisions within undertakings in Ghana.* Geneva: I.L.O., 1981.

596. Steel, W. F. "Female and small-scale employment under modernization in Ghana." *Economic Development and Cultural Change,* 30, 1 (October 1981), 153-67.

597. Date-Bah, E. *Sex inequality in an African urban labour market: the* *case of Accra-Tena*. Geneva: I.L.O., 1982. 82p.

598. International Labour Organisation. *Report of the National Tripartite Seminar on the development of labour relations in Ghana, 1980*. Geneva: I.L.O., 1982. 10p.

599. Hodsdon, D. F. *General Agricultural Workers' Union of the TUC (Ghana)*. Geneva: I.L.O., 1983. iii, 46p.

600. Sutton, I. "Labour in commercial agriculture in Ghana in the late nineteenth and early twentieth centuries." *Journal of African History*, 24, 4 (1983), 461-83.

See also 12, 79, 98, 141.

Greece

601. International Labour Organisation. *Labour problems in Greece*. London: Staples for the I.L.O., 1949.

602. Jecchinis, C. *Trade unionism in Greece: a study of political paternalism*. Roosevelt University, 1967.

603. Jecchinis, C. "The role of trade unionism in the social development of Greece." Kassalow, E. (ed.) *The role of trade unions in developing societies*. Geneva: International Institute for Labour Studies, 1978.

604. Industrial Relations Services. "Greece: industrial relations in a state of confusion." *European Industrial Relation Review*, 60 (January 1979), 17-18.

605. Industrial Relations Services. "Greece: Industrial relations in context." *European Industrial Relations Review*, 67 (August 1979), 6-7.

606. Industrial Relations Services. "Greece: recent collective bargaining developments." *European Industrial Relations Review*, 89 (June 1981), 6-7.

607. Economist. "Greek trade unions: tell us what to do." *Economist*, 282, 7228 (13th March 1982), 50-1.

608. Industrial Relations Services. "Greece: Trade union democracy law." *European Industrial Relations Review*, 103 (August 1982), 6-7.

609. Industrial Relations Services. "Greece: new law on equality." *European Industrial Relations Review*, 120 (January 1984).

610. Industrial Relations Services. "Greece: bargaining demands."

European Industrial Relations Review, 121 (February 1984).

611. Industrial Relations Services. "Greece: new central agreement." *European Industrial Relations Review*, 122 (March 1984).

612. Industrial Relations Services. "Greece: new national unemployment scheme." *European Industrial Relations Review*, 125 (June 1984).

613. Industrial Relations Services. "Greece: reforms in industrial relations law." *European Industrial Relations Review*, 127 (Auguat 1984).

614. Industrial Relations Services. "Greece: challenge to strike law." *European Industrial Relations Review*, 128 (September 1984).

615. Katsanevas, Theodore K. *Trade unions in Greece*. Athens: National Centre of Social Research, 1984. 283p.

Guatemala

616. Friedman, Jesse A. *Labor law and practice in Guatemala*. Washington: U.S.G.P.O., 1962. 32p.

617. Maddox, R. C. *Wage differences between United States and Guatemalan industrial firms in Guatemala*. Austin: Texas University, Bureau of Business Research, 1971. 57p.

618. Guatemala. Consejo Nacional de Planificacion Economica. *Documentos de trabajo sobre recursos humanos y empleo 1976-1980*. Guatemala: C.N.P.E., 1980. 53p.

619. Guatemala. Consejo Nacional de Planificacion Economica. *Planificacion de los recursos humanos y el empleo: documentos de trabajo*. Guatemala: C.N.P.E., 1980. Three volumes.

620. Guatemala. Consejo Nacional de Planificacion Economica. *Resena bibliografica sobre empleo en Guatemala*. Guatemala: C.N.P.E., 1983. ii, 77p.

Guinea

621. International Labour Organisation. Jobs and Skills Programme for Africa. *Manpower demand and supply in the agricultural sector of member states of the Mano River Union*. Addis Ababa: I.L.O., 1982.

See also 135.

Guyana

622. Newman, Peter. *British Guiana: problems of cohesion in an immigrant society.* Oxford: Oxford University Press, 1964.

623. Adamson, A. H. *Sugar without slaves.* Yale University Press, 1972.

624. Rodney, W. "Guyana: the making of the labour force." *Race and Class*, 22 (Spring 1981), 331-52.

Haiti

625. Leyburn, J. G. *The Haitian people.* Second edition. Yale University Press, 1966.

626. Nicholls, D. "Poorest nation of the Western world." *Geographical Magazine,* 50 (October 1977), 47-54.

627. Allman, J and May, J. "Fertility, mortality, migration and family planning in Haiti." *Population Studies,* 33 (November 1979), 505-21.

628. Lundahl, Mats. *Peasants and poverty: a study of Haiti.* London: Croom Helm, 1979.

629. Geggus, D. "The British government and the Saint Domingue slave revolt, 1791-1793." *English Historical Review,* 96 (April 1981), 285-305.

630. Haiti. Direction de la Planification Economique et Sociale. *Enquête sur l'emploi urbain en Haiti 1978-1979.* Port au Prince: La Direction, 1981. 108p.

Honduras

631. Szretter, H. *Honduras: el empleo en el Plan Nacional de Desarollo 1979-1983.* Santiago: I.L.O., 1980. vi, 116p.

632. International Labour Organisation. Regional Employment Programme for Latin America and the Caribbean. *Honduras: situacion y politicas de empleo en el Corto Plazo.* Santiago: I.L.O., 1983. vii, 99p.

Hong Kong

633. Hetherington, R. M. "Industrial labour in Hong Kong." *Hong Kong Economic Papers,* 2 (March 1963).

634. England, Joe. "Industrial relations in Hong Kong." Hopkins, K. (ed.) *Hong Kong: the industrial colony.* Oxford: Oxford University Press, 1971. p.242-3.

635. Ward, B. E. "A small factory in Hong Kong." Willmott, W. (ed.) *Economic organisation in Chinese society.* Stanford University Press, 1972. p.384-5.

636. Carr, Neil. "Employee attitude survey in a Hong Kong engineering company." *Journal of Industrial Relations,* 15(1) March 1973. p.108-11.

637. Easey, Walter. "Notes on child labour in Hong Kong." *Race and*

Class, 18 (Spring 1977), 377-87.

638. Morris, R. "Labour relations in the Hong Kong merchant navy." *Maritime Policy and Management*, 5, 2 (April 1978), 111.

639. England, Joe. "Trade unionism and industrial disputes in Hong Kong: an explanatory framework." Paper presented to the 1979 Asian Regional Conference on Industrial Relations, Tokyo.

640. England, Joe and Rear, John. *Industrial relations and law in Hong Kong*. Oxford: Oxford University Press, 1981. 421p.

641. Scott, Ian and Burns, John P. (eds.) *The Hong Kong Civil Service: personnel policies and practices*. Oxford: Oxford University Press, 1985. 352p.

See also 120.

Hungary

642. Haraszti, Miklos. *A worker in a workers' state*. Harmondsworth: Penguin, 1977.

643. Toth, A. E. *Some new economic and managerial features of small-scale agricultural production in Hungary*. Hungarian Academy of Sciences, Institute of Economics, 1978.

644. Hethy, Lajos. "Participation in Hungary." *Industrial Participation*, 568 (Autumn 1979), 27-32.

See also 69, 74, 88, 102, 123.

Iceland

645. Gronvold, Halldor. *The Federation of State and Municipal Employees' Unions (BSRB) and public sector industrial relations in Iceland.* Coventry: University of Warwick, 1982.

646. Olafsson, S. *Modernization and social stratification in Iceland.* Oxford: Oxford University, 1982.

India

647. Rao, A. V. Raman. *Collective bargaining versus government regulation: India and the USA.* Bombay: Allied Publishers, 1964.

648. Agarwal, R. D. *Dynamics of labour relations in India.* New York: McGraw-Hill, 1973.

649. Prasad, Lallan. *Personnel management and industrial relations in the public sector.* Delhi: Progressive Corporation, 1973.

650. John, C. K. *Incomes policy and industrial relations.* Shri Ram Centre, 1974.

651. Rao, A. V. Raman. *Labour-management relations.* D.K. Publishing, 1974.

652. Sharma, Balder Raj. *The Indian industrial worker.* Delhi: Vikas, 1974.

653. Banerjee, B. and Karbur, S. M. "On the specification and estimation of macro rural-urban migration functions: with an application to Indian data." *Oxford Bulletin of Economics and Statistics*, 43 (February 1981), 7-29.

654. Bardhan, P. and Rudra, A. "Terms and conditions of labour contracts in agriculture." *Oxford Bulletin of Economics and Statistics*, 43 (February 1981), 89-111.

655. Berry, Roger. "Redistribution, demand structure and factor requirements: the case of India." *World Development*, 9 (July 1981), 621-35.

656. Ramaswamy, E. A. and Ramaswamy, U. *Industry and labour: an introduction.* Oxford: Oxford University Press, 1981.

657. Reddy, Y. R. K. "Strikes in India." *Indian Journal of Industrial Relations*, 17, 2 (October 1981), 239-48.

658. Visaria, Pravin. "Poverty and unemployment in India: an analysis of recent evidence." *World Development,* 9 (March 1981), 277-300.

659. Broder, I. and Morris, C. "Socially weighted real income comparisons: an application to India." *World Development,* 10 (February 1982), 91-102.

660. Chellappa, H. and Jhuraney, J. C. "Cause of peace in industrial relations." *Indian Journal of Industrial Relations,* 18, 1 (July 1982), 1-28.

661. Dayal, Sahab. "Revival of collective bargaining in India: some recent evidence." *Indian Journal of Industrial Relations,* 17, 3 (1982), 319-37.

662. Saini, Debi S. "Industrial democracy: law and challenges in India." *Indian Journal of Industrial Relations,* 19, 2(October 1983), 191-206.

663. Sharma, B. R. and Rajan, P.S.S. "Organisational determinants of labour-management relations in India." *Indian Journal of Industrial Relations,* 19, 1 (July 1983), 1-20.

664. Usha, S. "Labour market discrimination against women." *Indian Journal of Industrial Relations,* 18, 4 (April 1983), 569-85.

665. Wood, John C. "An interesting judgement of the Supreme Court of India." *Industrial Relations Journal,* 15, 1 (Spring 1984), 94-7.

See also 25, 82, 106, 111, 112, 117, 128, 133, 149.

Indonesia

666. Wells, L. T. "Men and machines in Indonesia'a light manufacturing industries." *Bulletin of Indonesian Economic Studies,* 9, 3 (November 1973), 62-72.

667. Bekti, H. *Industrial relations in Indonesia and the role of PUSPI.* Geneva: I.L.O., 1974. 11p.

668. Jones, G. "What do we know about the labour force in Indonesia?" *Majalah Demografi Indonesia,* 2, 1 (December 1974), 7-36.

669. Natesan, V. R. and Mutatkar, V. A. *Indonesia: emploment injury insurance fund.* Geneva: I.L.O., 1974. 21p.

670. Arndt, H. W. and Sundrum, R. M. "Wage policies in Indonesia." *International Labour Review,* 112, 5 (November 1975), 369-87.

671. Berouti, L. *Employment and training patterns, problems and requirements in the manufacturing sector in Indonesia.* Jakarta: I.L.O., 1975. Two volumes.

672. Sundrum, R. M. "Manufacturing employment 1961-1971." *Bulletin of Indonesian Economic Studies,* 11, 1 (March 1975), 58-65.

673. Sethuraman, S. V. *Jakarta: urban development and employment.* Geneva: I.L.O., 1976. viii, 154p.

674. Wilkins, Nigel. "Indonesia's employment problem: the policy alternatives." *Asian Affairs,* 65 (June 1978), 168-78.

675. Harris, D. S. *Country labour profile: Indonesia.* Washington: U.S.G.P.O., 1979. 8p.

676. Moir, H. V. J. "Leknas labor utilization survey: some data on labor utilization from selected areas of Java." *Ekonomi don Keuangan Indonesia,* 22, 4 (December 1979), 423-46.

677. Peluso, N. L. *Putting people into boxes or building boxes around people? Approaches to designing occupational categories for Java.* Yogyakarta: Universitas Gadjah Mada, 1979. 34p.

678. Moir, H. V. J. "Female access to non-primary occupations: the Indonesian case." *Demografi Indonesia,* 14, 7 (December 1980), 50-75.

679. Hadiwardojo, O., Kodisin, K. and Soepadno, S. *Relations between workers and employers in Indonesia.* Geneva: I.L.O., 1981.

680. Indonesian Documentation and Information Centre, Leiden. *Indonesian workers and their right to organise.* Leiden: I.D.I.C., 1982. 148p.

681. Soemontri, S. *Study of Indonesia's economically active population.* Yogyakarta: Gadjah Mada University Press, 1982. xiii, 118p.

682. Strout, A. M. "Seasonal factors and rural employment on Java." *Ekonomi dan Keuangan Indonesia,* 30, 2 (June 1982), 149-86.

683. Clark, D. B. *How secondary school graduates perform in the labor market: a study of Indonesia.* Washington: International Bank for Reconstruction and Development, 1983. 69p.

684. Mather, C. E. "Industrialization in the Tangerang Regency of West Java: women workers and the Islamic patriarchy." *Bulletin of Concerned Asian Scholars,* 15, 2 (1983), 2-17.

See also 31, 145, 149.

Iran

685. Delaney, W. F. *Labor law and practice in Iran.* Washington: U.S.G.P.O., 1964.

686. Arasteh, A. R. *Man and society in Iran.* Leiden: Brill, 1970.

687. Yar-Shater, Ehsan (ed.) *Iran faces the seventies.* New York: Praeger, 1971.

688. International Labour Organisation. *Employment and incomes policies for Iran.* Geneva: I.L.O., 1973.

689. Fischer, A. J. "The labour market in Iran." *Contemporary Review,* 230 (April 1977), 209-12.

690. Kazemi, Farhad. *Poverty and revolution in Iran: the migrant poor, urban marginality and politics.* New York: New York University Press, 1980.

691. Van Ginneken, W. "Some methods of poverty analysis: an application to Iranian data, 1975-1976." *World Development,* 8 (September 1980), 639-46.

See also 25, 35.

Iraq

692. Sallas, Gustav A. *Labour law and practice in Iraq.* Washington: U.S.G.P.O., 1962.

693. Fattah, Zeki. "Development and structural change in the Iraqui economy and manufacturing industry: 1960-1970." *World Development,* 7 (August-Sepember 1979), 813-23.

Ireland

694. Hillery, Brian, Kelly, Aidan and Marsh, I. *Trade union organisation in Ireland.* Dublin: Irish Productivity Centre, 1975.

695. McCarthy, Charles. *Trade unions in Ireland, 1894-1960.* Dublin: Institute of Public Administration, 1977.

696. Gibson, Chris. "Centralised wage bargaining and industrial relations: the Irish experience." *Personnel Management,* 10, 9 (September 1978), 22-6.

697. Nevin, Donal (ed.) *Trade unions and change in Irish society.* Dublin: Mercier, 1980.

698.. Pollock, Hugh. "The Irish pattern of industrial relations." *Personnel Management*, 12, 5 (May 1980), 26-9.

699. Pollock, Hugh M. "Membership participation in a small trade union." *Studies*, 49 (Autumn-Winter 1980), 193-209.

700. Whelan, C. T. *Employment conditions and job satisfaction: the distribution, perception and evaluation of job rewards.* Dublin: Economic and Social Research Institute, 1980.

701. O'Hara, Bernard J. *The evolution of Irish industrial relations law and practice.* Dublin: Folens, 1981.

702. Pollock, Hugh M. (ed.) *Industrial relations in practice.* Dublin: O'Brien Press, 1981.

703. Greaves, Charles Desmond. *The Irish Transport and General Workers' Union: the formative years, 1909-1923.* Dublin: Gill & Macmillan, 1982.

704. Keogh, Dermot. *The rise of the Irish working class.* Belfast: Appletree, 1982.

705. Pollock, Hugh M. (ed.) *Reform of industrial relations.* Dublin: O'Brien Press, 1982.

706. Kelly, A. and Roche, W. "Institutional reform in Irish industrial relations." *Studies*, 72 (Autumn 1983), 221-30.

707. O'Farrell, P. N. "Components of manufacturing employment change in Ireland 1973-1981." *Urban Studies*, 21 (May 1984), 155-76.

See also 80.

Israel

708. Preuss, Walter. *The labour movement in Israel: past and present.* Jerusalem: Rubin Mass, 1965.

709. Metcalf, David. "Wage policy in Israel" *British Journal of Industrial Relations*, 8, 2 (July 1970), 213-23.

710. Lefkowitz, J. *Public employee unionism in Israel.* University of Michigan, Institute of Industrial and Labor Relations, 1971.

711. Rosenstein, Eliezer. "Workers' participation in management:

problematic issues in the Israeli system." *Industrial Relations Journal*, 8, 2 (Summer 1977), 55-69.

712. Chermesh, R. "Strikes: the issue of social responsibility." *British Journal of Industrial Relations*, 17, 3 (November 1979), 337-46.

713. Gidron, B. and Glaser, S. "Dealing with the problem of professional isolation in community work: the Iraeli experience." *Community Development Journal*, 14 (January 1979), 25-33.

714. Fischer, H. and Jacobsen, C. "Unauthorised strikes and slowdowns in Israel." *British Journal of Industrial Relations*, 20, 3 (November 1982), 342-8.

715. Wolkinson, B. J. and Cohen, A. "Use of work sanctions in Israeli labour disputes." *British Journal of Industrial Relations*, 20, 2 (July 1982), 231-46.

See also 21, 29, 62, 86, 130.

Italy

716. Sylos-Labini, Paolo. *Trade unions, inflation and productivity*. New York: Saxon House, 1974.

717. Spriano, Paolo. *The occupation of the factories*. London: Pluto Press, 1975.

718. Williams, Gwyn. *Proletarian order: Antonio Gramsci, factory councils and the origins of Italian communism, 1911-1921*. London: Pluto Press, 1975.

719. Farneti, Paolo. "The troubled partnership: trade unions and working class parties in Italy, 1948-78." *Government and Opposition*, 13 (Autumn 1978), 416-36.

720. Caloia, Angelo. "Industrial relations in Italy: problems and perspectives." *British Journal of Industrial Relations*, 17, 1 (March 1979), 259-68.

721. Low-Beer, J. R. *Protest and participation: the new working class in Italy*. Cambridge: Cambridge University Press, 1979.

722. Contini, B. "Labour market segmentation and the development of the parallel economy: the Italian experience." *Oxford Economic Papers*, 33 (November 1981), 401-12.

723. European Foundation for the Improvement of Living and Working

Conditions. *Right to information in union negotiations in Italy.* Dublin: The Foundation, 1981.

See also 14, 21, 52, 136, 140.

Ivory Coast

724. Roussel, L. *Côte d'Ivoire 1965: emploi.* Fontenoy-sous-Bois: Maind, 1968. 192p.

725. Achio, A. *Physionomie de l'emploi: Côte d'Ivoire 1968-1975.* Abidjon: Ivory Coast. Ministère du Plan, Direction des études de développement, 1969. iv, 542p.

726. Achio, F. *Taux de renouvellement des emplois qualifiés du secteur secondaire.* Abidjon: Ivory Coast. Office National de Formation Professionnelle, 1970. 26p.

727. Roussel, L. "Employment problems and policies in the Ivory Coast." *International Labour Review,* 104, 6 (December 1971), 505-25.

728. Ivory Coast. Office Nationale de Formation Professionnelle. *Secteur privé et para-public en Côte d'Ivoire 1971.* Abidjon: Ivory Coast. Ministère du Plan, 1971. Four volumes.

729. Achio, A. *Rémunerations: traitements et salaires en Côte d'Ivoire.* Abidjon: Direction des études de développement, 1972. 181p.

730. Ivory Coast. Ministère du Plan. *Problèmes de l'emploi 1965-2000.* Paris: Self, 1972, iii, 135p.

731. Ivory Coast. Ministère du Plan. *Emploi: valeurs de base: évolutions antérieures et tendances: modele dynamique.* Paris: Self, 1973. 234p.

732. France. Secretariat d'Etat aux Affaires Etrangeres. Direction de l'Aide au Développement. *Evolution des structures de l'emploi en Côte d'Ivoire, 1965-1971.* Paris: La Direction, 1974. vii, 85p.

733. Joshi, H., Lubell, H. and Mouly, J. *Urban development and employment in Abidjan.* Geneva: I.L.O., 1974.

734. Achio, A. *Structure des emplois et des rémunerations dans le secteur secondaire.* Abidjon: Direction Générale de la Planification, 1978. 160p.

735. Syndicat des Industriels de Côte d'Ivoire. *Barene des salaires minimaux.* Abidjon: Le Syndicat, 1979. 66p.

736. Pegatienan-hiey, J. *Salaires réels, productivité et emploi industriel.* Abidjon: Centre Ivoirien de Recherches Economiques et Sociales, 1979. 28p.

737. Achio, F. *Analyse des relations entre l'emploi et la formation et elaboration des politiques de formation: le cas de la Côte d'Ivoire.* Abidjon: Office Nationale de Formation Professionnelle, 1980. 37p.

738. Achio, F. *Conditions de travail et de vie des femmes dans les industries alimentaires en Côte d'Ivoire: le cas particulère des conserveries.* Geneva: I.L.O., 1981. 78p.

739. Gbayoro, K. and Robert, K. G. *Artisanat de service et de production en milieu rural: enquête regionale.* Abidjon: Office Nationale de Production en Milieu Rurale, 1981. 112p.

See also 28.

Japan

740. Dore, Ronald. *British factory - Japanese factory.* Berkeley: University of California Press, 1973.

741. Mire, J. "Workers' morale in Japan." *Monthly Labor Review,* 98, 6 (June 1975), 49-53.

742. Hanami, T. A. "The lifetime employment system in Japan: its reality and future." *Atlanta Economic Review,* 26, 3 (May-June 1976), 35-40.

743. Inoue, K. "From labour surplus to labour shortage economy: the case of Japan." *International Labour Review,* 113, 2 (March-April 1976), 217-26.

744. Tachiban, T. "Quality change in labour input: Japanese manufacturing." *Review of Economics and Statistics,* 58, 3 (1976), 293-9.

745. Clarke, O. "Industrial relations: some insights from Japan." *OECD Observer,* 86 (May 1977), 23-6.

746. Levine, S. B. and Taira, K. "Labour markets, trade unions and social justice?" *Japanese Economic Studies,* 5, 3 (Spring 1977), 66-92.

747. Marshall, B. K. "Japanese business ideology and labor policy." *Columbia Journal of World Business,* 12, 1 (Spring 1977), 22-30.

748. Ministry of Labour (Japan). *Labour problems in Japan: on the recent employment situation.* Tokyo: Foreign Press Center, 1977. 20p.

749. Nikon, Keizai. *The future of labour problems in Japan.* Tokyo: Japan Economic Research Center, 1977.

750. Organisation for Economic Co-operation and Development. *The development of industrial relations systems: some implications of Japanese experience.* Paris: O.E.C.D., 1977. 56p.

751. Yakabe, Hatsumi. *Labor relations in Japan: fundamental characteristics.* Tokyo: Japan Ministry of Foreign Affairs, 1977. 86p.

752. Haitani, K. "Changing characteristics of Japanese employment system." *Asian Survey,* 18, 10 (1978), 1029-45.

753. Ito, Koicai. "Industrial structure and labor in 1990." *Japan Economic Journal,* 16, 790-792 (March 14th 1978), 24-.

754. Koike, Kazuo. "Internal labour markets and industrial relations systems on the shop floor in Japan." *Keizai Kagatu,* 25, 3 (February 1978), 1-29.

755. Levine, S. B. and Taira, K. "Japanese industrial relations: is one economic miracle enough?" *Monthly Labor Review*, 101, 3 (1978), 31-3.

756. Lincoln, J. R., Olson, J. and Hamada, M. "Cultural effects on organizational structure: the case of Japanese firms in the United States." *American Sociological Review*, 43, 6 (1978), 829-47.

757. Pascale, R. T. "Zen and the art of Management." *Harvard Business Review*, 56, 2 (March-April 1978), 153-63.

758. Atsumi, R. "Tsukiai: obligatory personal relationships of Japanese white-collar company employees." *Human Organisation*, 38, 1 (1979), 63-70.

759. Cole, R. E. *Work, mobility and participation: a comparative study.* Berkeley: University of California Press, 1979.

760. Hanami, T. "Japan." Blanpain, R. (ed.) *International Encyclopedia for Labour Law and Industrial Relations.* Kluwer, 1981. Volume 7.

761. Jacoby, S. "Origins of internal labor markets in Japan." *Industrial Relations*, 18, 2 (Spring 1979), 184-96.

762. Japan Institute of Labour. *Employment and employment policy.* Tokyo: The Institute, 1979.

763. Japan Institute of Labour. *Labor unions and labor-management relations.* Tokyo: The Institute, 1979.

764. Kazama, Run. *Some observations on basic problems of the popular spring labor offensive: for fresh development of the Japanese trade union movement.* Kanto Gakuin University, 1979.

765. Kuniyosai, Urabe. "A critique of theories of the Japanese style management system." *Japan Economic Studies*, 7, 4 (Summer 1979), 33-41.

766. Ministry of Labour (Japan). *Japan's labour economics 1978: a summary.* Tokyo: Foreign Press Center, 1979. 41p.

767. Pucik, V. "Lifetime employment in Japan: alternative to the culture-structure causal model." *Journal of International Affairs*, 33, 1 (1979), 158-61.

768. Shiba, T. "Personal savings function of urban worker households in Japan." *Review of Economics and Statistics*, 61, 2 (1979), 206-13.

769. Fruin, W. M. "The family as a firm and the firm as a family: the

case of Kikkoman-Shoyu-Company Ltd." *Journal of Family History*, 5, 4 (1980), 432-49.

770. Furuya, K. I. "Labor-management relations in post-war Japan: their reality and change." *Japan Quarterly*, 27, 1 (1980), 29-38.

771. Hamada, T. "Winds of change: economic realism and Japanese labour management." *Asian Survey*, 20, 4 (1980), 397-406.

772. Nakao, T. "Wages and market power in Japan." *British Journal of Industrial Relations*, 18, 3 (November 1980), 365-8.

773. Nishiyama, Shunsaitu. *The labor market in Japan: selected readings*. Tokyo: University of Tokyo Press, 1980. 277p.

774. Tanaka, H. "Low growth and aging labor force." *Japan Quarterly*, 27, 1 (1980), 39-45.

775. Tomoko, Hamaha. "Winds of change: economic realism and Japanese labor management." *Asian Survey*, 20, 4 (April 1980), 397-407.

776. Ujihara, Shojiro. "Enterprise-based labor unions in Japan." *Annals of the Institute of Social Science*, 21 (1980), 1-23.

777. Yamamoto, Kiyoshi. "Labor-management relations at Nissan Motor Co. Ltd. (Datsun)." *Annals of the Institute of Social Science*, 21 (1980), 24-43.

778. Drucker, Peter F. "Behind Japan's success." *Harvard Business Review*, 59, 1 (January-February 1981), 83-90.

779. Goldstein, S. G. M. "Involving managers in system improvement planning." *Long Range Planning*, 14, 1 (February 1981), 93-9.

780. Kagono, T., Nonaka, I., Okumura, A., Sarakibara, K., Komatsu, Y. and Sarasaita, A. "Mechanistic US organic management systems: a comparative study of adaptive patterns in US and Japanese firms." *Annals of Business Administration*, 25 (1981), 115-45.

781. Lincoln, J. R., Hamada, M. and Olson, J. "Cultural orientations and individual reactions to organisations: a study of employees of Japanese owned firms." *Administrative Science Quarterly*, 26, 1 (1981), 93-115.

782. Rehder, R. R. "What American and Japanese managers are learning from each other." *Business Horizons*, 24, 2 (1981), 63-70.

783. Yamamotu, Kiyoshi. "Mass demonstration movements in Japan in the period of post-war crisis." *Capital and Class*, 12 (Winter 1980-1981),

5-36.

784. Dore, Ronald. "Goodwill and the spirit of market capitalism." *British Journal of Sociology*, 34 (December 1983), 459-82.

785. Ford, G. W. "Japan as a learning society." Lansbury, R. D. (ed.) *Managing industrial conflict*. Macquarie University, 1983.

786. Inoue, K. *Structural changes and labour market policies*. Geneva: I.L.O., 1983.

787. Kuwahara, Y. "Technological change and industrial relations in Japan." *Bulletin of Comparative Labour Studies*, 12 (1983).

788. Shirai, T. "Is Japan a conflict free society?" Lansbury, R. D. (ed.) *Managing industrial conflict*. Macquarie University, 1983.

789. Kendall, Walter. "Why Japanese workers work." *Management Today*, (January 1984), 72-5.

790. Shirai, T. "Recent trends in collective bargaining in Japan." *International Labour Review* 123, 3 (May-June 1984), 307-18.

See also 23, 90, 134, 149.

Jordan

791. Jordan: Department of Statistics. *Wages and salaries in the private sector 1970*. Ahman: The Department, 1971. 71p.

792. Jordan. Department of Statistics. *Employment survey for establishments engaging 5 persons or more*. Ahman: The Department, 1980.

793. Mujahid, G. B. S. *Female labour force participation in the Hashemite Kingdom of Jordan*. Beirut: I.L.O., 1982. 62p.

794. International Labour Organisation. *Jordan: comprehensive population and manpower policy*. Geneva: I.L.O., 1983. iv 264p.

See also 26.

Kenya

795. Amsden, A. H. *The international firm and labour in Kenya: 1945-70.* London: Cass, 1971.

796. International Labour Organisation. *Employment, incomes and equality: a strategy for increasing productive employment in Kenya.* Geneva: I.L.O., 1972.

797. Clayton, A. and Savage, D. *Government and labour in Kenya 1895-1963.* London: Cass, 1974.

798. Muir, J. D. "Labour legislation in industrial disputes: the Kenyan case." *British Journal of Industrial Relations,* 13, 3 (November 1975), 334-45.

799. Sandbrook, R. *Proletarians and African capitalism: the Kenyan case.* Cambridge: Cambridge University Press, 1975.

800. Henley, John S. "The personnel profesionals of Kenya." *Personnel Management,* 9, 2 (February 1977), 10-14.

801. Mulvey, Charles. "A note on the impact of unionization on negotiated wages in the manufacturing sector in Kenya." *Oxford Bulletin of Economics and Statistics,* 39 (August 1977), 229-31.

With a reply by W. J. House and Henry Rempel, 233-5.

802. Hazlewood, A. "Kenya: income distribution and poverty: an unfashionable view." *Journal of Modern African Studies,* 16 (1978), 81-95.

803. Henley, J. S. "Pluralism, underdevelopment and trade union power: evidence from Kenya." *British Journal of Industrial Relations,* 16, 2 (July 1978), 224-42.

804. Henley, J. S. and House, W. J. "The changing fortunes of an aristocracy? Determination of wages and conditions of employment in Kenya." *World Development,* 6 (January 1978), 83-95.

805. House, W. J. and Killick, Tony. "Hodd on income distribution in Kenya: a critical note." *Journal of Development Studies,* 14 (April 1978), 370-4.

With a reply by M. Hodd, 375-7.

806. House, W. J. and Rempel, H. "Labour market pressures and wage determination in less developed economies: the case of Kenya." *Economic Development and Cultural Change,* 26, (April 1978), 609-19.

807. Collier, P. and Bigsten, A. "A model of educational expansion and labour market adjustment applied to Kenya." *Oxford Bulletin of Economics and Statistics*, 43 (February 1981), 31-49.

808. House, William J. "Redistribution, consumer demand and employment in Kenyan furniture-making." *Journal of Development Studies*, 17 (July 1981), 336-56.

See also 19, 98, 108, 110, 112.

Korea, North

809. Korea. Ministry of Science and Technology. *Third five-year manpower development plan 1972-76.* Seoul: The Ministry, 1971. 75p.

810. Hollander, E. D. *Role of manpower in Korean economic development.* Seoul: Communications Media, 1972.

811. Woo, K. D. "Labour force, wage level and economic growth in Korea." *Asian Economics*, 2 (September 1972), 12-51.

812. Tak, H. J. "Study on the minimum wage system in Korea." *Asian Economics*, 4 (March 1973), 26-43.

813. Park, Y. K. *Labor and industrial relations in Korea: system and practice.* Seoul: Sogang University, Institute for Labour and Management, 1974. 160p.

814. Shin, H. "Industrial relations system in Korea: what should be done?" *Asian Economics*, 8 (March 1974), 5-26.

815. Whang, J. H. *Industrial relations in the Republic of Korea and the role of the Korean Employers' Association.* Geneva: I.L.O., 1974. 6p.

816. Caldwell, Malcolm. "North Korea: aspect of a new society." *Contemporary Review*, 233 (December 1978), 281-9.

817. Rao, D. C. "Economic growth and equity and the Republic of Korea." *World Development*, 6 (March 1978), 383-96.

818. Harris, D. S. *Country labour profile: Republic of Korea.* Washington: U.S.G.P.O., 1979. 4p.

819. Bognano, M. F. and Kim, S. "Collective bargaining in Korea." Industrial Relations Research Association. *Proceedings*, 1981. p.193-201.

820. International Labour Organisation and Korea. Ministry of Labour.

Proceedings of the PIACT National Tripartite Seminar on Occupational Safety and Health, Seoul, 1981. Seoul: P.I.A.C.T. and I.L.O., 1981. 402p.

821. Christian Conference of Asia. Urban Rural Mission. *From the womb of Han: stories of Korean women workers.* Hong Kong: C.C.A., 1982. 92p.

822. International Labour Organisation and Korea. National Institute of Labour Science. *Project findings and recommendations.* Geneva: I.L.O., 1983. 33p.

Korea, South

823. United States. Bureau of Labor Statistics. *Labor law and practice in the Republic of Korea.* Washington: U.S.G.P.O., 1969. 45p.

824. Kim, I. S. *Pour l'amélioration et le renforcement du travail des organisations de travailleurs.* Pyongyang: Editions en Langues Etrangères, 1972. 23p.

825. Ro, Y. K., Adams, D. W. and Hushak, L. J. "Income instability and consumption: savings in South Korean farm households 1965-70." *World Development,* 9 (February 1981), 183-91.

826. Jae Wan Chung. "Inflation in a newly industrialised country: the case of Korea." *World Development,* 10 (July 1982), 531-9.

See also 24, 120.

Kuwait

827. Al Moosa, Addulrasool and McLachlan, Keith. *Immigrant labour in Kuwait.* London: Croom Helm, 1985. xi, 208p.

Laos

828. Pollak, Morris. *Labour law and practice in the Kingdom of Laos.* Washington: U.S.G.P.O., 1965. 59p.

829. Vaidya, K. G. and Sarma, M. T. R. *Assessment of labour availability in the Lao People's Democratic Republic.* Geneva: I.L.O., 1984. 38p.

Lebanon

830. Clarke, Joan. *Labor law and practice in Lebanon.* Washington: U.S.G.P.O., 1966. 98p.

831. Maroun, J. *Liban: prévisions sur les besoins en main-d'oeuvre et les besoins en formation: rapport.* Beyrouth: Ministère du Plan, 1966. 306p.

832. Berouti, L. *Problèmes de l'emploi au Liban.* Beyrouth: Université saint-Joseph, 1968. 1038p.

833. Chidiac, R. *Salaire en droit positif libannais.* Beyrouth: Librairie du Liban, 1972. 320p.

834. Berouti, L. *Crise de l'emploi au Liban.* Beyrouth: Université Libanaise, 1973.

835. Bashir, I. "Training for the public sector in Lebanon." *Revue Internationale des Sciences Administratives*, 40, 4 (1974), 359-65.

836. Hamoudi, Q. *Applications des conventions et récommendations internationales du travail par les états arabes: contribution á la théorie du droit international des relations de travail.* Lille: Université de Lille, 1974. iv, 321p.

837. Beirut University College. Institute for Women's Studies in the Arab World. *Women and work in Lebanon.* Beirut: The Institute, 1980. 85p.

838. Zeinaty, A. "Seminar for working women in Lebanon." *Labour Education*, 45 (1981), 11-13.

Lesotho

839. Gordon, E. "An analysis of the impact of labour migration on the lives of women in Lesotho." *Journal of Development Studies*, 17 (April 1981), 59-76.

See also 50, 58, 108, 144.

Liberia

840. Yadi, M. *Employment promotion problems in the economic and social development of Liberia.* Geneva: International Institute for Labour Studies, 1972. 48p.

841. Liberia. Ministry of Planning and Economic Affairs. *Projection of total employment and manpower requirements in Liberia, 1972-1982.* Monrovia: The Ministry, 1973. 20p.

842. Stewart, R. S. M. *Assessment of unemployment in Liberia.* Monrovia: Ministry of Planning and Economic Affairs, 1973. 24p.

843. Akerlele, O. Women and the fishing industry in Liberia: measures of women's participation. Addis Ababa: U.N. Economic Commission for Africa, 1979. xi, 82p.

844. Bonaparte, T. H. "Multinational corporations and culture in Liberia." *American Journal of Economics and Sociology,* 38 (July 1979), 237-51.

845. Akpa, E. K. "Size distribution of income in Liberia." *Review of Income and Wealth,* 27, 4 (December 1981), 387-400.

846. Campbell, E. K. *Differential participation of men and women in the active labour force in urban Liberia.* Monrovia: [Privately printed], 1981. 48p.

847. International Labour Organisation. *Improvement and development of the employment service.* Geneva: I.L.O., 1981. 50p.

848. International Labour Organisation. *Report of the National Tripartite Seminar on the Development of Labour Relations in Liberia, Monrovia, 1982.* Geneva: I.L.O., 1982. 6p.

See also 12, 135, 148.

Libya

849. Nair, A. *Libya's manpower resources and educational and training needs 1964-71.* Tripoli: Libyan Ministry of Labour and Social Affairs, 1967. 120p.

850. International Labour Organisation. *Libya: industrial vocational* *training scheme: report on project results, conclusions and recommendations.* Geneva: I.L.O., 1973. ii, 60p.

851. Wedley, W. C. "Libya: super-rich, labor-poor." *Columbia Journal of World Business,* 9, 2 (Summer 1974), 64-74.

852. International Labour Organisation. *Libya: establishment of an apprentice scheme.* Geneva: I.L.O., 1975. 24p.

853. International Labour Organisation. *Socialist Peoples Libyan Arab Jamahiriya: a report on manpower, productivity and organisational aspects of development.* Geneva: I.L.O., 1980. ii, 55p.

854. International Labour Organisation. *Memorandum to the government of the Libyan Arab Jamahiriya on wage policy and pay administration practices and occupational classification and job evaluation for the public sector.* Geneva: I.L.O., 1981. 225p.

855. Sankari, F. A. "Oil, human values and the development syndrome: the Libyan case." *Studies in Comparative International Development,* 16, 1 (Spring 1981), 53-74.

856. International Labour Organisation. *Socialist People's Libyan Jamahiriya: occupational safety.* Geneva: I.L.O., 1982. 13p.

Luxembourg

857. Organisation for Economic Co-operation and Development. *Manpower policy in Luxemburg.* Paris: O.E.C.D., 1970. 149p.

858. Stoffels, J. *Syndicalisme au Luxembourg et en Europe.* Luxembourg: Université Internationale des Sciences Comparées, 1972. 339p.

859. European Communities. *Social security for migrant workers: Luxembourg.* Luxembourg: E.C., 1975. 52p.

860. Schintgen, R. *Legislation du travail au Grand-Duche de Luxembourg.* Luxembourg: Ministère du Travail et de la Securité Sociale, 1976. 374p.

861. European Foundation for the Improvement of Living and Working Conditions. *Santé et securité sur le lieu de travail: Luxembourg.* Dublin: The Foundation, 1979.

862. European Foundation for the Improvement of Living and Working Conditions. *Shiftwork in the service sector: Luxembourg.* Dublin: The Foundation, 1981.

863. Schintgen, R. *Participation des travailleurs aux décisions dans l'entreprise au Grand-Duche de Luxembourg.* Geneva: I.L.O., 1981. 18p.

864. European Foundation for the improvement of Living and Working Conditions. *Shiftwork in the chemical industry: surveys: Luxembourg.* Dublin: The Foundation, 1982.

865. European Foundation for the Improvement of Living and Working Conditions. *Wage payment systems: Luxembourg.* Dublin: The Foundation, 1982.

866. European Foundation for the Improvement of Living and Working Conditions. *Survey of Research on Working Time and Leisure Time: Luxembourg.* Dublin: The Foundation, 1983.

867. Luxembourg. Service Central de la Statistique et des Etudes Economiques. *Recensement de la population du ... 1981.* Luxembourg: La Service, 1984.

Includes employment statistics.

See also 17.

Malawi

868. Page, M. E. "Land and labor in rural Malawi." *Rural Africana*, 20 (Spring 1973), 1-68; 21 (Summer 1973), 1-66.

869. International Institute for Labour Studies. *Labour problems in the economic and social development of Malawi.* Geneva: I.I.L.S., 1975. 39p.

870. Chipeta, C. "Wage determination and the cost-effectiveness of alternative labour systems in smallholder agriculture." *Eastern African Journal of Rural Development*, 12, 1-2 (1979), 152-72.

871. Kydd, J. and Christiansen, R. "Structural change in Malawi since independence: consequences of a development strategy based on large-scale agriculture." *World Development*, 10 (May 1982), 355-75.

872. Chipande, G. H. R. *Labour availability and smallholder agricultural development: the case of Lilongare Land Development Programme, Malawi.* Geneva: I.L.O., 1983. iii, 85p.

873. Christiansen, R. and Kydd, J. "The return of Malawian labour from South Africa and Zimbabwe." *Journal of Modern African Studies*, 21 (June 1983), 311-26.

See also 144, 147.

Malaysia

874. Gamba, C. *Origins of trade unionism in Malaya: a study in colonial labour unrest.* Singapore: Eastern Universities Press, 1962. xx, 511p.

875. Malaya. Department of Statistics. *Report on employment and unemployment in metropolitan towns.* Kuala Lumpur: The Department, 1966. 44p.

876. Kumaran, K. K. *Collective bargaining in the rubber industry.* Petaling Jaya: National Union of Plantation Workers, 1967. 42p.

877. Malayan Employers' Consultative Association. *Study on terms and conditions of service.* Kuala Lumpur: The Association, 1969. 14p.

878. Malaysia. Economic Planning Unit. *Second Malaysian Plan 1971-75: trained manpower requirements for agricultural development.* Kuala Lumpur: The Unit, 1970. 96p.

879. Stenson, M. R. *Industrial conflict in Malaya: prelude to the communist revolt of 1948.* Oxford: Oxfrod University Press, 1970.

880. Wheeler, A. C. R. *Manpower problems and prospects, Saba, 1969.* Kota Kinabalu: Ministry of Finance, 1970.

881. Mehmet, O. "Job vacancy survey as a tool of labour market information in developing countries." *Relations Industrielles,* 26, 3 (August 1971), 692-707.

882. Nijhar, K. S. "Employment opportunities under the second Malaysian plan, and the role of the Malaysian Trade Union Congress." *Ekonomi,* 12, 1 (1971), 85-104.

883. Mehmet, O. "Manpower planning and labour markets in developing countries: a case study of West Malaysia." *Journal of Development Studies,* 8, 2 (January 1972), 277-88.

884. Thillainathan, R. "Second Malaysian plan: issues relating to the employment strategy." *Ekonomi,* 12, 2 (1972), 6-14.

885. Vaura, Z. *Labour force projections by race, sex and age for West Malaysia, 1970-1995.* Bergen: Chr. Michelsen Institute, 1972. viii, 141p.

886. Rudner, M. "Malayan labor in transition: labor policy and trade unionism, 1955-63." *Modern Asian Studies,* 7, 1 (January 1973), 21-45.

887. Snyder, D. L. *Report to the government of Malaysia on the development of the Manpower Department in the Ministry of Labour and Manpower.* Geneva: I.L.O., 1973. 20p.

888. Fernando, W. *Industrial relations in Malaysia and the role of the Malayan Agricultural Producers Association.* Geneva: I.L.O., 1974. 4p.

889. Seang, N. K. *Industrial relations in Malaysia and the role of the Malayan Employers' Consultative Association.* Geneva: I.L.O., 1974. 3p.

890. Malaysian Trades Union Congress. *Industrial relations in Malaysia.* Petaling Jaya: M.T.U.C., 1975. xiv, 233p.

891. Munch-Petersen, P. M. *Report to the government of Malaysia on labour market information.* Geneva: I.L.O., 1975. 7p.

892. Solomon, D. *Urbanisation and employment in Kuala Lumpur.* Geneva: I.L.O., 1975. xviii, 142p.

893. Morgan, Michael. "The rise and fall of Malayan trade unionism 1945-50." Amin. M. and Caldwell, M. (eds.) *Malaya: the making of a neo-colony.* Nottingham: Spokesman, 1977.

894. Chin, Y. L. *Country paper on industrial relations and development*

(Malaysia). Kuala Lumpur: Ministry of Labour and Manpower, 1978.

895. Muzumdar, D. and Ahmed, M. *Labour market segmentation and the determination of earnings: a case study.* Washington: International Bank for Reconstruction and Development, 1978. 37p.

896. Liat, C. Y. *Industrial relations and development in Malaysia.* Bangkok: I.L.O., 1979.

897. Canlas, D. B. and Razak, M. *Education and the labour force participation of married women: West Malaysia 1970.* Quezon City: Council for Asian Manpower Studies, 1980. 46p.

898. Chan, P. "Forgotten little people: a study of urban child labour in a developing economy." *Asian Economics*, 35 (December 1980), 67-79.

899. Harris, D. S. *Country labour profile: Malaysia.* Washington: U.S.G.P.O., 1980. 6p.

900. Henley, J. S. "State management of labour relations in industrialising economies." *Indian Journal of Industrial Relations*, 16, 1 (July 1980), 25-43.

901. Moir, H. "Alternative frameworks for assessing labour utilization: policy implications and some illustrative data from Java." *Malayan Economic Review*, 25, 1 (April 1980), 62-81.

902. Siwar, C and Alias, M. H. J. "Underutilization of labour in agriculture: a survey of concepts and empirical measures for Malaysia," *South East Asian Economic Review*, 1, 2 (August 1980), 153-64.

903. Fan, N. H. *Preliminary study of women rubber estate workers in peninsular Malaysia.* Geneva: I.L.O., iii, 45p.

904. Halim, F. "Rural labour force and industrial conflict in West Malaysia." *Journal of Contemporary Asia.*, 11, 3 (July-September 1981), 271-96.

905. International Labour Organisation. *Memorandum to the government of Malaysia on public sector manpower planning.* Geneva: I.L.O., 1981. ii, 58p.

906. Malaysia. Ministry of Labour and Manpower. *Labour and manpower report 1980.* Kuala Lumpur: The Ministry, 1981. 233p.

907. Menon, K. A. *Conciliation and arbitration in Malaysia.* Geneva: I.L.O., 1981. 5p.

908. Nazumdar, D. *Labor market and income distribution: a study of*

Malaysia. New York: Oxford University Press, 1981. xvi, 375p.

909. Hirschman, C. "Unemployment among urban youths in peninsular Malaysia, 1970: a multivariate analysis of individual and structural effects." *Economic Development and Cultural Change*, 30, 2 (January 1982), 391-412.

910. Leppel, K. "Relations among child quality, family structure and the value of the mother's time in Malaysia." *Malaysian Economic Review*, 27, 2 (October 1982), 61-70.

911. Mehmet, O. "Malaysian employment restructuring policies: effectiveness and prospects under the fourth Malaysian plan, 1980-85." *Asian Survey*, 22, 10 (October 1982), 978-87.

912. Halim, F. "Workers' resistance and management control: a comparative case study of male and female workers in West Malaysia." *Journal of Contemporary Asia*, 13, 2 (1983), 131-50.

See also 3, 31, 41, 55, 133.

Mali

913. Mali. Direction Nationale de la Statistique et de l'Informatique. *Recensement général de la population, 1976*. Bamako: La Direction, 1980.

   Includes employment statistics.

914. Mali. Regional Economic Research and Documentation Center. *Trade unionism in the Republic of Mali: case study*. Lome: The Center, 1983. 78p.

See also 107.

Malta

915. Royal University of Malta. Department of Economics. *Alternative industrial relations systems for Malta*. The Department, 1971.

916. Koziara, E. C. *The labour market and wage determination in Malta*. Royal University of Malta, 1975.

917. Milne, Robin G. "Unemployment in Malta 1956-71." *Journal of Development Studies*, 12 (July 1976), 383-95.

Mauritania

918. International Labour Organisation. *Memorandum au gouvernement de Mauritanie sur la politique des salaires.* Geneva: I.L.O., 1978. 19p.

See also 107.

Mexico

919. American Chamber of Commerce of Mexico. *Mexican labor contracts 1968.* Mexico City: The Chamber, 1968. 42p.

920. Perrakis, S. *Wage differentials in a labour surplus economy: the case of Mexico.* Berkeley: university of California Press, 1970. v, 360p.

921. Healy, R. G. "Effects of improved housing on worker performance." *Journal of Human Resources*, 6, 3 (Summer 1971), 297-308.

922. Isbister, J. "Urban employment and wages in a developing economy: the case of Mexico." *Economic Development and Cultural Change*, 20, 1 (October 1971), 24-46.

923. Levenstein, H. A. *Labor organizations in the United States and Mexico: a history of their relations.* Westport: Greenwood, 1971. x, 258p.

924. Arie, C. G. *De los seguros sociales a la seguridad social.* Mexico City: Editorial Parrua, 1972.

925. Blum, A. A. and Thompson, M. "Unions and white-collar workers in Mexico." *Industrial and Labor Relations Review*, 26, 1 (October 1972), 646-59.

926. Perrakis, S. "The labour-surplus model and wage behaviour in Mexico." *Industrial Relations*, 11, 1 (February 1972), 80-95.

927. Clarke, M. R. *Organized labor in Mexico.* New York: Russell & Russell, 1973. 315p.

928. Germidis, Dimitrios A. *Labour conditions and industrial relations in the building industry in Mexico.* Paris: O.E.C.D., 1974. 149p.

929. International Labour Organisation. "Labour administration and employment policies: conclusions of a technical seminar held in Mexico." *International Labour Review*, 110, 5 (November 1974), 423-36.

930. McFarland, E. L. *Employment growth in services: Mexico 1950-*

1969. New York: Columbia University, Faculty of Political Science, 1974. ix, 688p.

931. Stevens, Evelyn P. *Protest and response in Mexico*. Cambridge, Mass.: M.I.T. Press, 1974. 372p.

932. Watanabe, S. "Constraints on labour-intensive export industries in Mexico." *International Labour Review*, 109, 1 (January 1974), 23-45.

933. Baerresen, C. W. "Unemployment and Mexico's border industrialization program.8U *Inter-American Economic Affairs*, 29, 2 (Autumn 1975), 79-90.

934. Gregory, P. "Impact of institutional intervention on industrial wages in Mexico." Industrial Relations Research Association. *Proceedings*, 28 (1975), 24-31.

935. Schlagheck, James L. *The political, economic and labor climate in Mexico*. Philadelphia: University of Pennsylvania, Wharton School, Industrial Research Unit, 1977. 164p.

936. Lowenstein, M. R. *Profile of labor conditions: Mexico*. Washington: U.S.G.P.O., 1979. 8p.

937. Jimenez, M. T. *Caracteristicas de la demanda de mano de obra femenina en sectores seleccianadas de la industria de transformacias*. Mexico City: Institut Nacional de Estudias del Trabajo, 1979. 185p.

938. Reynolds, C. W. "Labor market projections for the United States and Mexico and current migration controversies." *Food Research Institute Studies*, 17, 2 (1979), 121-55.

939. Corzo, Ramirez R. *Approche théoretique pour l'étude du syndicalisme mexicain pendant 1970-1976*. Paris: Université de Paris VIII, 1980. 426p.

940. Schlagheck, J. L., Johnson, N. R. and Hemphill, G. F. *Political, economic and labour climate in Mexico*. Philadelphia: University of Pennsylvania, Wharton School, Industrial Research Unit, 1980. x, 186p.

941. Arizpe, L. and Apanda, J. "Comparative advantage of women's disadvantages: women workers in the strawberry export agribusiness in Mexico." *Signs*, 7, 2 (Winter 1981), 453-73.

942. Cervantes, Compos P. *Apuntamientos para una teoria del proceso laboral*. Mexico City: Secretaria de Trabajo y Prevision Social, 1981. 117p.

943. Chavez, A. R. *Mexico: conciliation and the system of labour* *administration.* Geneva: I.L.O., 1981. 4p.

944. Mexico. Centro Nacional de Productividad. *Sistema de relaciones laborales: libros de consulto.* Mexico City: C.N.P., 1982. Ten volumes.

945. Mexico. Comision Consultiva del Empleo y la Productividad. Subcomision de Recursos Humanos. *Proyecto para la planificacion de recursos humanos: informe final.* Mexico City: C.C.E.P., 1982. vii, 461p.

946. Pommier, P. "Place of Mexico City in the nation's growth: employment trends and policies." *International Labour Review,* 121, 3 (May-June 1982), 345-60.

947. Thompson. M. and Roxborough, I. "Union elections and democracy in Mexico." *British Journal of Industrial Relations,* 20, 2 (July 1982), 201-17.

948. Astarga, Lira E. and Commander, S, *Mexico: commercialisation and the growth of a migratory labour market.* Geneva: I.L.O., 1983. iii, 49p.

949. Fernandez-Kelly, M. P. *For we are sold, I and my people: women and industry in Mexico's frontier.* Albany: State University of New York Press, 1983. vii, 217p.

950. Prevot-Schapira, M. F. "Evolution de l'organisation syndicale mexicaine." *Notes et Etudes Documentaires,* 4731-2 (23rd September 1983), 79-104.

951. Roxborough, I. and Eizberg, I. "Union locals in Mexico." *Journal of Latin American Studies,* 15, 1 (May 1983), 117-35.

952. Zapata, F. "Conflits du travail au Mexique depuis 1934," *Notes et Etudes Documentaires,* (23rd September 1983), 107-22.

See also 7, 23, 61.

Morocco

953. Andriamananjara, R. *Labor mobilization: the Moroccan experience.* Ann Arbor: Michigan University, Center for Research on Economic Development, 1971. vi 119p.

954. Assime, A. "Comment peut-on envisager une solution aux problèmes posés par l'utilisation des resources humaines au Maroc?" *Bulletin Economique et Social du Maroc,* 126 (January 1975), 33-46.

955. Morocco. Ministère du Travail et des Affaires Sociales. *Maroc au travail.* Rabat: La Ministère, 1975. 97p.

956. Van Rijokeghen, W. *Employment problems and policies in developing countries: the case of Morocco.* Rotterdam: Rotterdam University Press, 1976. 211p.

957. Morocco. Direction de la Statistique. *Résultats de l'enquête sur l'emploi urbain.* Rabat: La Direction, 1978. 112p.

958. Merson, B. *Country labour profile: Morocco.* Washington: U.S.G.P.O., 1980. 8p.

959. Ayache, A. *Mouvement syndical au Maroc.* Paris: Editions l'Hamatton, 1982.

Covers the period 1919-42.

See also 108, 109, 141.

Mozambique

960. First, R. and Manghezi, A. *Black gold: the Mozambican miner, proletarian and peasant.* Brighton: Harvester, 1983. xxxi, 256p.

See also 18, 22.

Namibia

961. Kane-Berman, J. *Contract labour in South West Africa*. Johannesburg: South African Institute of Race Relations, 1972. 37p.

962. Von Konrat, G. *Passport to truth: inside South West Africa: an astounding story of oppression*. London: W. H. Allen, 1972. xiii, 241p.

963. Fraenkel, P. *Namibians of South West Africa*. London: Minority Rights Group, 1974. 48p.

964. Gordon, Robert J. *Mines, masters and migrants: life in a Namibian mine compound*. Johannesburg: Raven Press, 1977.

965. Wilks, B. S., Anderson, J. E., Baurmann, R. and Midgaad, S. *Analysis of the main aspects of manpower and education needs for Namibia in a situation of transition to majority rule*. Washington: African-American Scholars Council, 1977. 66p.

966. Duggal, N. K. (ed.) *Manpower estimates and development implications for Namibia*. Lusaka: U.N., Institute for Namibia, 1978. 72p.

967. Cronje, Gillian and Cronje, Suzanne. *The workers of Namibia*. International Defence and Aid Fund for Southern Africa, 1979. 135p.

968. International Labour Organisation. *Analysis of legislative and other changes required to eliminate discrimination in labour matters and to promote conformity with international labour standards in an independent Namibia*. Geneva: I.L.O., 1981. ii, 78p.

969. Melber, H. "National Union of Namibian Workers: background and formation." *Journal of Modern African Studies*, 21, 1 (March 1983), 151-8.

See also 22.

Nepal

970. Blaikie, M. P., Cameron, J. and Seddon, J. *The struggle for basic needs in Nepal*. Paris: O.E.C.D., 1980.

See also 82, 128, 133.

Netherlands

971. Windmuller, John P. *Labor relations in the Netherlands*. Ithaca, New York: Cornell University Press, 1969. 469p.

972. Albeda, W. "Recent trends in collective bargaining in the Netherlands." International Labour Organisation. *Collective bargaining in industrialized market economies.* Geneva: I.L.O., 1974. p.315-36.

973. Kendall, Walter. "The Netherlands." Kendall, Walter *The labour movement in Europe.* London: Allen Lane, 1975. p.242-78.

974. Lijphart, Arend. *The politics of accomodation: pluralism and democracy in the Netherlands.* London: University of California Press, 1975. 231p.

975. Akkermans, Tinie and Grootings, Peter. "From corporatism to polarisation: elements of the development of Dutch industrial relations." Crouch, Colin and Pizzorno, Alessandro (eds.) *The resurgence of class conflict in Western Europe since 1968.* Volume 1: *National Studies.* London: Macmillan, 1978. p.159-89.

976. Vries, Johan de. *The Netherlands economy in the twentieth century.* Assen: Van Gorcum, 1978. 135p.

977. Vliet, G. E. van. *Bedrijvenwerk als vorm van belangenbehartiging.* Alphen aan den Rijn: Samson, 1979. 594p.

With an English summary.

978. Fase, W. J. P. M. *Vijfendertig jaar loonbeleid in Nederland.* Alphen aan den Rijn: Samson, 1980. 676p.

With an English summary.

979. Griffiths, Richard T. (ed.) *The economy and politics of the Netherlands since 1945.* The Hague: Nijhoff, 1980. 311p.

980. Andriessen, Eric. "The Dutch industrial relations system." Industrial Democracy in Europe, International Research Group. *European industrial relations.* Oxford: Clarendon Press, 1981. p.138-63.

981. Bakels, H. L. "The Netherlands." Blanpain, Roger (ed.) *The international encyclopedia for labour law and industrial relations.* Volume 7, number 4. Deventer: Kluwer, 1982. 84p.

982. Peper, Bram and Kooten, Gerrit van. "The Netherlands: from an ordered harmonic to a bargaining relationship." Barkin, Solomon (ed.) *Worker militancy and its consequences: the changing climate of Western industrial relations.* New York: Praeger, 1983. p.111-46.

983. Windmuller, John P., Galan, C. de and Zweeden, A. F. van. *Arbeidsverhoudingen in Nederland.* Utrecht: Spectrum, 1983. 470p.

Updated version of *Labor relations* (1969).

984. Voorden, William van. "Employers association in the Netherlands." Windmuller, John P. and Gladstone, Alan (eds.) *Employers associations and industrial relations.* Oxford: Clarendon Press, 1984. p.202-31.

985. Albeda, W. "Recent trends in collective bargaining in the Netherlands." *International Labour Review,* 124, 1 (January-February 1985), 49-60.

See also 13, 38, 47, 127.

New Zealand

986. Roth, Herbert. *Trade unions in New Zealand, past and present.* Reed Education, 1973.

987. Howells, John M., Woods, Noel S. and Young, F. (eds.) *Labour and industrial relations in New Zealand.* Pitman, 1974.

988. Woods, Noel S. *Industrial relations: a search for understanding.* Hicks Smith, 1975.

989. Deeks, John. "Ideology and industrial relations in New Zealand." *New Zealand Journal of Industrial Relations,* 1, 2 (August 1976), 26-31.

990. Holt, James. "The political origins of compulsory arbitration: a comparison with Great Britain." *Journal of New Zealand History,* 19 (October 1976), 99-111.

991. Turkington, Don. *Industrial conflict: a study of three New Zealand industries.* Methuen, 1976.

992. Young, John."New Zealand industrial relations: retrospect and prospect." *New Zealand Journal of Industrial Relations,* 1, 1 (May 1976), 3-7.

993. Deeks, John. "Trade unions and politics in New Zealand." *New Zealand Journal of Industrial Relations,* 2, 1 (May 1977), 9-15.

994. Geare, Alan. "Final offer arbitration: a critical examination of the theory." *Journal of Industrial Relations,* 19, 4 (1977), 373-85.

995. Turkington, Don. "The trend of strikes in New Zealand." *Journal of Industrial Relations,* 19, 3 (1977), 286-95.

996. Deeks, John (and others). *Industrial relations in New Zealand.*

Methuen, 1978.

997. Smith, David F. "A critique of worker participation in New Zealand." *New Zealand Journal of Industrial Relations*, 3, 2 (August 1978), 71-8.

998. Gill, Howard. "Legislated apathy: industrial relations in New Zealand." *New Zealand Journal of Industrial Relations*, 4, 3 (November 1979), 7-14.

999. Smith, David F. "Developments in worker participation in New Zealand." *Journal of Industrial Relations*, 21, 1 (1979), 35-50.

1000. Holt, James. "Compulsory arbitration in New Zealand, 1894-1901." *New Zealand Journal of Industrial Relations*, 5 (October 1980), 179-200.

1001. Harbridge, R. J. (ed.) *Challenge or disaster? Industrial relations in the 1980s*. Victoria: Victoria University of Wellington, Industrial Relations Centre, 1981.

1002. Smith, David and Turkington, Don. *A profile of voluntary collective bargaining in New Zealand*. Victoria: Victoria University of Wellington, Industrial Relations Centre, 1981.

1003. Wilson, Margaret A. "Recent developments in New Zealand's industrial relations system." *New Zealand Journal of Industrial Relations*, 6 (April 1981), 35-41.

1004. Bolger, J. B. "The government's role in industrial relations." *New Zealand Journal of Industrial Relations*, 7 (April 1982), 35-7.

1005. Harbridge, R. J. (ed.) *Industrial relations: further insights*. Victoria: Victoria University of Wellington, Industrial Relations Centre, 1982.

1006. Harbridge, R. J. (ed.) Industrial relations: insights and directions. Victoria: Victoria University of Wellington, Industrial Relations Centre, 1982.

1007. Roper, K. "The impact of the Remuneration Act 1979-1980." *New Zealand Journal of Industrial Relations*, 7 (April 1982), 1-12.

1008. Binnie, K. and Smith, D. "Managerial unionism and the law in New Zealand." *New Zealand Journal of Industrial Relations*, 9 (August 1984), 69-80.

1009. Endres, Tony. "The New Zealand full employment goal: a survey of changing views 1950 to 1980." *New Zealand Journal of Industrial*

Relations, 9 (April 1984), 33-44.

See also 36, 118.

Nigeria

1010. Yesufu, Tijani Momodu. *An introduction to industrial relations in Nigeria.* Oxford: Oxford University Press, 1965. 190p.

1011. Ananaba, Wogu. *The trade union movement in Nigeria.* London: Hurst, 1969. 336p.

1012. Akpala, A. "Labour policies and practices in Nigeria." *Journal of Industrial Relations,* 13, 3 (September 1971), 274-90.

1013. Etukudo, Akanimo Jonathan. *Multi-employer bargaining: industrial relations system in the banking industry in Nigeria.* Ilfracombe: Stockwell, 1971. 252p.

1014. Iwuji, E. C. *Employment promotion problems in the economic and social development of Nigeria.* Geneva: International Institute for Labour Studies, 1972. 61p.

1015. Nigeria. National Manpower Board. *Labour force sample survey, 1966-67.* Lagos: The Board, 1972.

1016. Nigeria. National Manpower Board. *Survey of manpower shortages and surpluses, 1968-69.* Lagos: The Board, 1973. 71p.

1017. Nigeria. National Manpower Board. *University graduate employment: a sample survey of employment experience amongst Nigerian men and women graduating in 1972.* Lagos: The Board, 1973.

1018. Rimlinger, G. V. and Stremlau, C. C. *Indigenisation and management development in Nigeria.* Lagos: Nigerian Institute of Management, 1973. 110p.

1019. Cohen, Robin. *Labour and politics in Nigeria, 1945-71.* London: Heinemann, 1974. 302p.

1020. Fapohunda, C. J. *Characteristics of the unemployed people in Lagos.* Lagos: Lagos University, Human Resources Research Unit, 1974. iii, 50p.

1021. Orimalade, O. O. *Bibliography on labour in Nigeria, 1910-1970.* Lagos: National Library of Nigeria, 1974. xvi, 267p.

1022. Yesufu, T. M. "Employment, manpower and economic

development in Nigeria: some issues of moment." *Nigerian Journal of Economic and Social Studies*, 16, 1 (March 1974), 49-63.

1023. Etukudo, Akanimo Jonathan. *Waging industrial peace in Nigeria*. Hicksville, N.Y.: Exposition Press, 1977.

1024. Nigeria. National Manpower Board. *Study of Nigeria's manpower requirements, 1977.* Lagos: The Board, 1979. 117p.

1025. Waterman, Peter. *Wage labour relations in Nigeria: state capitalists, unions and workers in the Lagos cargo-handling industry.* The Hague: Institute of Social Studies, 1979.

    Available on microfiche from Inter Documentation.

1026. Adeogun, A. A. "Strikes: the law and the institutionalization of labour protest in Nigeria." *Indian Journal of Industrial Relations*, 16, 1 (July 1980), 1-23.

1027. Fashoyin, T. *Industrial relations in Nigeria.* London: Longman, 1980. x, 166p.

1028. Harris, D. S. and Rabiu, B.I.O. *Country labour profile: Nigeria.* Washington: U.S.G.P.O., 1980. 8p.

1029. Aderinto, A. "Labour mobility in Nigeria: patterns and implications for balanced development." *Labour and Society*, 6, 2 (April-June 1981), 163-79.

1030. Bello, J. A. and Iyanda, O. *Appropriate technology choice and employment creation by two multinational enterprises in Nigeria.* Geneva: I.L.O., 1981. iii, 37p.

1031. Bosah, J. I. O. *Conciliation in industrial disputes in Nigeria.* Geneva: I.L.O., 1981. 5p.

1032. Fashayin, T. *Industrial relations and the political process in Nigeria.* Geneva: International Institute for Labour Studies, 1981. vii, 59p.

1033. Fashoyin, T. "State regulation of trade disputes in essential services in Nigeria." *Relations Industrielles*, 36, 1 (1981), 207-22.

1034. Manu, E. D. "Transfer of technology to small scale farmers in Nigeria." *Eastern Africa Journal of Rural Development*, 14, 1 (1981), 237-47.

1035. Nwabueze, R. O. "Impact of military rule on Nigerian trade union movement (1966-1978)." *Indian Journal of Industrial Relations*, 16, 4

(April 1981), 571-92.

1036. Otobo, D. "Nigerian general strike of 1981." *Review of African Political Economy*, 22 (October-December 1981), 65-81.

1037. Olukoya, A. I., Bademosi, M. A. and Williams, F. O. *Workers' participation in decisions within undertakings in Nigeria: recent trends and problems.* Geneva: I.L.O., 1981. 20p.

1038. International Labour Organisation. *Report of the National Tripartite Seminar on the Development of Labour Relations in Nigeria, 1981.* Geneva: I.L.O., 1982. 11p.

1039. Pestoff, V. A. *Role of Trade unions and consumer co-operatives in the development of Nigeria: a preliminary overview.* Stockholm: Stockholm University, 1982. 72p.

1040. Ahiauzu, A. I. "Cultural influences on managerial industrial relations policies: a note on Hausa and the workplaces in Nigeria." *Labour and Society*, 8, 2 (April-June 1983), 151-62.

1041. Ekechukwu, T. O. "Collective bargaining and processes of settling industrial disputes in Nigeria." *Indian Journal of Industrial Relations*, 18, 4 (April 1983), 607-12.

1042. International Labour Organisation. *Labour-management relations in public enterprises in Africa.* Geneva: I.L.O., 1983. 84p.

1043. Okafar, F. C. "Rural employment diversification in Anambra State, Nigeria: its nature and implications for development" *Labour, Capital and Society*, 16, 2 (November 1983), 226-39.

1044. Adeokun, L.A., Adepoju, A., Ilari, F. A. and Adewuyi, A. A. *Ife labour market: a Nigerian case study.* Geneva: I.L.O., 1984. 72p.

1045. Ahiauzu, Augustine. "Culture and workplace industrial relations: a Nigerian study." *Industrial Relations Journal*, 15, 3 (Autumn 1984), 53-63.

1046. Oribabor, Patrick E. "Recent trends in collectivbe bargaining in Nigeria." *Industrial Relations Journal*, 15, 4 (Winter 1984), 47-55.

1047. Pittin, Renee. "Documentation and analysis of the invisible work of invisible women: a Nigerian case study." *International Labour Review*, 123, 4 (July-August 1984), 473-90.

See also 12, 79, 98, 141, 148.

Norway

1048. Galenson, Walter. *Labour in Norway.* New York: Russell& Russell, 1970. 373p.

1049. Braun, K., Kahl, A. and Groemping, F. A. *Labor law and practice in Norway.* Washington: U.S.G.P.O., 1972. viii, 84p.

1050. Organisation for Economic Co-operation and Development. *Manpower policy in Norway.* Paris: O.E.C.D., 1972. 241p.

1051. Goss, John. *Industrial relations and employee participation in management in Norway.* Brighton: University of Sussex, Centre for Contemporary European Studies, 1973. 36p.

1052. Balfour, C. "Industrial relations in Norway." *Industrial Relations Journal,* 5, 2 (Summer 1974), 46-54.

1053. Norway. Arbeidsdirektoratet. *Labour market problems and programmes in Norway.* Oslo: The Author, 1974. 186p.

1054. Norway. Komiteen for Internasjonale Sosialpolitiske Saker. *Labour relations in Norway.* Oslo: K.I.S.S., 1975. 192p.

1055. Nygaard, K. and Bergo, C. T. "Trade unions: new users of research." *Personnel Review,* 4, 2 (Spring 1975), 5-10.

1056. Bolweg, Joep F. *Job design and industrial democracy: the case of Norway.* Leiden: Nijhoff, 1976. 139p.

1057. Emery, Fred and Thorsrud, Einar. *Democracy at work: the report of the Norwegian industrial democracy program.* Leiden: Nijhoff, 1976. 177p.

1058. Inman, John." Wages policy in Norway." *British Journal of Industrial Relations,* 17, 3 (November 1979), 347-61.

1059. Korsnes, Olav. "Duality in the role of unions and unionists." *British Journal of Industrial Relations,* 17, 3 (November 1979), 362-75.

1060. Mire, J. *Country labour profile: Norway.* Washington: U.S.G.P.O., 1979. 8p.

1061. Foss, O. *Attitudes and behaviour in the labour market.* Oslo: Statistisk Sentralbyra, 1980. 220p.

1062. Gustavsen, B. "From satisfaction to collective action: trends in the development of research and reform in working life." *Economic and Industrial Democracy,* 1, 2 (May 1980), 147-70.

1063. Norway. Direktoratet for Arbeidstilsynet. *Act of 4th February 1977 relating to worker protection and working environment as subsequently amended*

1064. Norway. Kommunal- og Arbeidsdepartmentet. *Employment and working conditions in the 1980s: perspectives on the significance of the technological and economic development for employment and working conditions.* Oslo: The Author, 1980. 102p.

1065. Nygaard, K. *Computer in the workplace: lessons from Norwegian experience.* Wellington: Victoria University of Wellington, Industrial Relations Centre, 1980. vi 15p.

1066. Fridstrom, L. *Labour force projections 1979-2000.* Oslo: Statistisk Sentralbyra, 1981. 109p.

1067. Gustavsen, Bjorn and Hunnius, Gerry. *New patterns of work reform: the case of Norway.* Oslo: Universitetsforlaget, 1981. 207p.

1068. Industrial Relations Services. "Norway: industrial relations in context part 1: a centralised system." *European Industrial Relations Review*, 84 (January 1981), 13-15.

1069. Industrial Relations services. "Norway: a working environment project." *European Industrial Relations Review*, 90 (July 1981), 20-21.

1070. International Labour Organisation. *Workers' participation in decisions within undertakings: an overview of the situation in Norway.* Geneva: I.L.O., 1981. 22p.

1071. Norway. Arbeidstilsynet. *Working Environment Act and the Annual Holidays Act.* Oslo: The Author, 1981. 20p.

1072. Norway. Statistisk Sentralbyra. *Women's work 1980.* Oslo: The Author, 1981. 111p.

1073. Hansen, H. O. and Ivarson, J. R. *Labour relations in Norway.* Geneva: I.L.O., 1982. 17p.

1074. Industrial Relations Services. "Norway: basic argument revised." *European Industrial Relations Review*, 101 (June 1982), 13-14.

1075. Industrial Relations Services. "Norway: new technology and data protection." *European Industrial Relations Review*, 106 (November 1982), 12-14.

1076. Industrial Relations Services. "Norway: pay round assessed." *European Industrial Relations Review*, 105 (October 1982), 7-8.

1077. Industrial Relations Services. "Norway: employment protection reform plans." *European Industrial Relations Review*, 114 (July 1983), 10-12.

1078. International Labour Organisation. *Trade union situation and labour relations in Norway.* Geneva: I.L.O., 1983. 53p.

1079. Lie, S. S. "Immigrant women and their work: a study of British, Yugoslavian and Chilean women in Norway." *Scandinavian Journal of Development Alternatives*, 2, 3 (September 1983), 51-75.

See also 13, 76, 80, 99, 127, 154.

Pakistan

1080. Farooq, G. M. and Winston, G. C. *Shift working, employment and economic development: a study of industrial workers in Pakistan.* Williamstown, Mass.: Williams College, Center for Development Economics, [n.d.]

1081. Pakistan. Central Statistical Office. *Population and labour force in Pakistan, 1964.* Karachi: C.S.O., 1966. xii, 102p.

1082. Karwanski, R. A. *Education and supply of manpower in Pakistan.* Karachi: National Commission on Mnapower and Education, 1970. xiii, 188p.

1083. Shafi, M. *Handbook of West Pakistan minimum wages legislation.* Karachi: Bureau of Labour Legislations, 1970. 84p.

1084. Usman, M. "Labour unrest: genesis and solutions." *Pakistan Management Review*, 11, 1 (Spring 1970), 68-75.

1085. Zar, Z. *Human resource planning, development and utilisation: a collection of reports and research papers.* Karachi: National Manpower Council, 1971. ix, 210p.

1086. Ahmed, I. *Unemployment and underemployment in Pakistan.* Ames: Iowa State University, 1972. iv, 596p.

1087. Ali, S. "Concepts of new industrial relationship in Pakistan." *Pakistan Management Review*, 13, 4 (October-December 1972), 94-100.

1088. Bhutto, Zulfikar Ali. *New deal for labour.* Karachi: President's Office, 1972. 23p.

1089. Haidari, I. *New labour policy: impact and implications.* Karachi: Economic and Industrial Publications, 1972. 92p.

1090. Usmani, U. R. "Changing patterns of labour policy in Pakistan." *Pakistan Management Review*, 13, 4 (October-December 1972), 45-63.

1091. Beg, M. A. "Review of labour force participation rates in Pakistan." *Pakistan Development Review*, 12, 4 (1973), 393-406.

1092. Pakistan. Planning Commission. *Labour and employment in Pakistan.* Karachi: The Commission, 1973. 56p.

1093. Rizvi, S. A. S. *Industrial labour relations in Pakistan.* Karachi: National Institute of Social and Economic Research, 1973. 76p.

1094. Shafi, M. *Handbook of Punjab minimum wages for 36 industries.* Karachi: Bureau of Labour Publications, 1973. iv, 132p.

1095. Shafi, M. *Punjab industrial relations rules, 1973.* Karachi: Bureau of Labour Publications, 1973. 32p.

1096. Shafi, M. *Sind industrial relations rules, 1973.* Karachi: Bureau of Labour Publications, 1973. 40p.

1097. Ahmed, K. S. *Industrial relations and the role of the Employers Association of Pakistan.* Geneva: I.L.O., 1974. 5p.

1098. Ashraf, Q. "Technical manpower development." *Pakistan Management Review*, 15, 1 (January-March 1974), 37-41.

1099. Husain, I. "Employment aspects of industrial growth in West Pakistan." *Pakistan Development Review*, 13, 1 (Summer 1974), 211-21.

1100. Husain, I. *Employment strategy for the 5th plan: some policy alternatives.* Karachi: [n.p.], 1974. 42p.

1101.. Mir, I. *Human resources development and utilization.* Lahore: Directorate of Labour Welfare, 1974. xv, 209p.

1102. Munim, M. A. "Problems in implementing new labour laws and suggestions to overcome them." *Pakistan Management Review*, 16, 3 (July-September 1974), 9-20.

1103. Shafi, M. *Industrial relations ordinance 1969 incorporating latest amendments...* Karachi: Bureau of Labour Publications, 1974. 66p.

1104. Shafi, M. *North West Frontier Province industrial relations rules, 1974.* Karachi: Bureau of Labour Publications, 1974. 32p.

1105. Shafi, M. *West Pakistan factory rules.* Karachi: Bureau of labour Publications, 1974. 61p.

1106. Shafi, M. *West Pakistan industrial and commercial employment (standing orders) ordinance 1968: commentary.* Karachi: Bureau of Labour Publications, 1974. 32p.

1107. Hafeez, S. "Problems of trade unions in Pakistan: an empirical reassessment." *Pakistan Management Review*, 16, 2 (April-June 1975), 103-9.

1108. Hafeez, S. "Problems of trade unions in Pakistan as perceived by their federations: an empirical assessment." *Pakistan Management Review*, 16, 3 (July-September 1975), 31-8.

1109. International Labour Organisation. *Technical memorandum to the government of Pakistan on manpower promotion and employment planning.* Geneva: I.L.O., 1975. 22p.

1110. Khan, B. A. "Notes on trade unionism in Pakistan." *Pakistan Management Review*, 16, 3 (July-September 1975), 21-30.

1111. Khan, D. *Growth of trade unions in North West Frontier Pakistan.* Peshawar: Peshawar University, Board of Economic Enquiry, 1975. 128p.

1112. Pakistan. Ministry of Labour and Works. Manpower Division. *Manpower planning: proceedings of a seminar.* Islamabad: The Ministry, 1975. xi, 209p.

1113. International Labour Organisation. *Towards an employment strategy in Pakistan.* Geneva: I.L.O., 1976.

1114. Pakistan National Federation of Trade Unions. *First Sind Tripartite Labour Conference.* Karachi: P.N.F.T.U., 1976. 27p.

1115. Bhutto, J. A. *Labour management relations in public enterprises in Pakistan.* Karachi: [Privately printed], 1977. 82p.

1116. Shaheed, Z. A. *Organisation and leadership of industrial labour in Karachi.* Leeds: Leeds University, Department of Politics, 1977. xii, 532p.

1117. Shafi, M. *Shafi's profit bonus: law and practice.* Karachi: Bureau of Labour Publications, 1976. iv, 30p.

1118. Risvi, S. A. S. *Industrial relations and development in Pakistan.* Bangkok: I.L.O., 1979. 68p.

1119. Ghafoar, A. "Institutional set-up of labour market in Pakistan." *Pakistan Labour Gazette*, (October-December 1980), 5-20.

1120. Khan, B. A. *Trade unionism and industrial relations in Pakistan.* Karachi: Royal Book Co., 1980. vii, 70p.

1121. Irfan, M. *Pakistan's labour force, its size and structure: a review of evidence.* Islamabad: Pakistan Institute of Development Economics, 1981. 55p.

1122. Pakistan. Ministry of Information and Broadcasting. *Pakistan: Labour and employment.* Islamabad: The Ministry, 1981. 30p.

1123. Pakistan. Ministry of Labour, Manpower and Overseas Pakistanis. *Study of the occupational and educational manpower requirements and supply of the 5th five-year plan, 1978-83.* Islamabad: The Ministry, 1981. 115p.

1124. Amjad, R. and Mahmood, K. *Industrial relations and the political* *process in Pakistan, 1947-77.* Geneva: International Institute for Labour Studies, 1982. vii, 61p.

1125. De Silva, S. R. *Leave, holidays and overtime in the private sector.* Colombo: Employers Federation of Ceylon, 1982. viii, 63p.

1126. Irfan. M. "Wages, employment and trade unions in Pakistan." *Pakistan Development Review,* 21, 1 (Spring 1982), 49-68.

1127. Khan, M. D. "Workers' participation in management: Pakistan's experience." *Pakistan Labour Gazette,* 57, 10-12 (October - December 1982), 1-22.

1128. Mirza, M. "Collective bargaining and settlements." *Industrial Relations Journal (Karachi),* 2, 4-6 (April-June 1982), 23-29, 41.

1129. Pakistan. Ministry of Labour, Manpower and Overseas Pakistanis. "Minimum wages in Pakistan." *Pakistan Labour Gazette,* 56 (July-September 1982), 15-24.

1130. Employers' Federation of Pakistan and International Labour Organisation. *Seminar for employers on working conditions, occupational safety and health and workers' welfare, Lahore and Karachi, 1983.* Karachi: I.L.O., 1983. iii, 90p.

1131. Rashdi, A. "Industrial disputes and their settlements in Pakistan." *Industrial Relations Journal (Karachi),* 3, 5-6 (May-June 1983), 39-49.

1132. Rural Development Foundation of Pakistan and International Labour Organisation. *National Workshop on rural non-farming activities for men and women for employment and income generation.* Islamabad: Ministry of Local Government and Rural Development, 1984. 80p.

See also 1, 35, 82, 128.

Panama

1133. International Labour Organisation. *Situacion y perspectivas del empleo en Panama.* Santiago: I.L.O., 1973. Four volumes.

1134. International Labour Organisation. *Situacion y perspectivas del empleo en Panama.* Geneva: I.L.O., 1974. xxi, 359p.

1135. International Labour Organisation. *Impacto de las inversiones publicas en el empleo en Panama.* Santiago: I.L.O., 1976. v, 156p.

1136. Hoffmann, H. and Sciara, A. J. *Diagnostico de las estadisticas y bibliografica sobre el empleo rural en Centroamerica y Panama.* Santiago: I.L.O., 1979.

1137. Bloem, P. *Centroamerica y Panama: archivo de datos occupacionales en el sector industrial.* Santiago: I.L.O., 1980. 44p.

1138. Harris, D. S. *Country labour profile: Panama.* Washington: U.S.G.P.O., 1980. 8p.

1139. Garcia Martinez, S. *Participacion de los trabajadores en las decesiones dentro las empresas en la Republica de Panama.* Geneva: I.L.O., 1981.

1140. International Labour Organisation. *Informe al gobierno de Panama sobre el mejoramiento de las condiciones y del medio ambiente de trabajo.* Geneva: I.L.O., 1982. vi, 97p.

1141. International Labour Organisation. Regional Employment Programme for Latin America and the Caribbean. *Panama: segmentacion del mercado de trabajo.* Geneva: I.L.O., 1982. iv, 210p.

Papua New Guinea

1142. Langmore, John and Berry, Roger. "Wages policy in Papua New Guinea." *Journal of Industrial Relations*, 20, 3 (1978), 293-302.

1143. Plowman, D. "Some aspects of trade union development in Papua New Guinea." *Australian Outlook*, 33 (December 1979), 326-38.

1144. Fitzpatrick, Peter. *Law and state in Papua New Guinea.* New York: Academic Press, 1980.

See especially chapter 6: "The working class."

Paraguay

1145. Monaghan, Jane. "Poverty in paradise." *Illustrated London News*, 265 (August 1977), 52-3.

Peru

1146. Payne, James L. *Labour and politics in Peru.* Yale University Press, 1965.

1147. Kruijt, D. and Vellinga, M. *Labour relations and multinational corporations: the Cerro de Pasco Corporation in Peru (1902-1974).* Assen: Van Gorcum, 1979. 262p.

1148. Guillet, D. "Surplus extraction, risk management and economic change among Peruvian peasants." *Journal of Development Studies,* 18 (October 1981), 3-24.

1149. Scott, C. D. "Agrarian reform and seasonal employment in coastal Peruvian agriculture." *Journal of Development Studies,* 17 (July 1981), 282-306.

1150. Ferner, Anthony. *La burguesia industrial en el desarrollo Peruano.* Lima: Editorial Esan, 1982.

1151. Brass, Tom. "Agrarian reform and the struggle for labour-power: a Peruvian case study." *Journal of Development Studies,* 19 (April 1983), 368-89.

See also 7.

Philippines

1152. International Labour Organisation. *Employment problems and policies in the Philippines.* Geneva: I.L.O., 1969.

1153. Mangahas, M., Meyers, W. H. and Barker, R. *Labour absorption in Philippine agriculture.* Paris: O.E.C.D., 1972.

1154. Ramos, E. T. *Philippine labour movement in transition.* Quezon City: New Day, 1976.

1155. Werz, R., Rodgers, G. and Hopkins, M. "Population, employment and poverty in the Philippines." *World Development,* 6 (April 1978), 519-32.

1156. Lindsey, C. W. "Size, structure, turnover and mobility of the largest manufacturing firms in a developing country." *Journal of Industrial Economics,* 29 (December 1979), 189-200.

1157. Ahammed, C. and Herdt, R. "Measuring the impact of consumption linkages on the employment effects of mechanisation in Philippine rice production." *Journal of Development Studies,* 20 (January 1984), 242-55.

See also 55, 134, 153, 158.

Poland

1158. Reynolds, Jaime. "Communists, socialists and workers: Poland 1944-48." *Soviet Studies*, 30 (October 1978), 516-39.

1159. MacShane, Denis. *Solidarity*. Nottingham: Spokesman, 1981.

1160. Raina, Peter. *Independent social movements in Poland*. London: London School of Economic and Political Science, 1981. 632p.

1161. Staniszkis, J. "The evolution of forms of working class protest in Poland." *Soviet Studies*, 33 (April 1981), 204-31.

1162. Taylor, John. *Five months with Solidarity*. New York: Wildwood House, 1981.

1163. Pravda, Alex. "Poland 1980: from "premature consumerism" to labour solidarity." *Soviet Studies*, 34 (April 1982), 167-99.

See also 69, 74, 88, 102, 123.

Portugal

1164. Bye, Basil and Doyle, Mel. *Workers in Europe: Portugal*. Workers' Educational Association, 1976.

1165. Goodey, Chris (and others). *Workers' control in Portugal*. Nottingham: Institute for Workers' Control, 1976.

See also 14.

Puerto Rico

1166. Friedlander, Stanley l. *Labor migration and economic growth: a case study of Puerto Rico*. Cambridge, Mass.: M.I.T. Press, 1965.

1167. Reynolds, Lloyd G. *Wages, productivity and industrialization in Puerto Rico*. New York: Irwin, 1965.

1168. Mintz, S. W. *Worker in the cane: a Puerto Rican life history*. New Haven: Greenwood press, 1974.

1169. Quintero Rivera, Angel. *Workers' struggles in Puerto Rico: a documentary history*. New York: Monthly Review Press, 1976.

1170. City of New York. Center for Puerto Rican Studies. *Labor migration under capitalism: the Puerto Rican experience*. New York: Monthly Review Press, 1979.

1171. Morris, Lydia. "Women without men: domestic organisation and the welfare state as seen in a coastal community of Puerto Rico." *British Journal of Sociology*, 30 (September 1979), 322-40.

1172. Santiago, C. and Thorbecke, E. "Regional and technological dualism: a dual-dual development framework applied to Puerto Rico." *Journal of Development Studies*, 20 (July 1984), 271-89.

Romania

1173. Petric, A. *L'unification du mouvement ouvrier de Roumanie.* Bucharest: Academie de la République Socialiste de Roumanie, 1967. 188p.

1174. Uniunea Generala a Sindicatelar din Romania. *Congrès de l'Union Generale des Syndicats de République Socialiste de Roumanie, 1971.* Bucharest: U.G.S.D.R., 1971. 231p.

1175. Taigar, S. "Some aspects of manpower utilisation policy in Romania. *Bulletin of the International Institute for Labour Studies,* 9 (1972), 91-8.

1176. Cernea, M. "Individual motivation and labour turnover under socialism." *Studies in Comparative International Development,* 8, 3 (Fall 1973), 303-23.

1177. Florescu, M. "Protection de la femme dans le droit du travail de la République Sociale de Roumanie." *Revue Romaine des Sciences Sociales,* 17, 1 (1973), 47-54.

1178. Romania. Ministreul Muncii. *Congrès Mondiale de Prévention des Accidents du Travail et des Maladies Professionnelles, 1977, Bucharest.* Bucharest: Ministreul, 1978.

Special emphasis on Romania.

1179. Chelcea, S., Marginean, I., Stefanescu, S. and Zamfir, C. *Dezvoltarea umana a intreprinderi.* Bucharest: Editura Academiei, 1980. 329p.

Humanisation of work.

1180. Nelson, D. "Workers in a workers' state: participation in Romania." *Soviet Studies,* 32 (October 1980), 542-60.

1181. Wehrenfennig, A. "Nuova namativa salariale in Romania." *Est-Ouest,* 15, 1 (1984), 7-13.

Samoa

1182. Pitt, David. *Tradition and economic progress in Samoa: a case study of the role of traditional social institutions in economic development.* Oxford: Clarendon Press, 1970.

1183. Firth, S. "Governors versus settlers: the dispute over Chinese labour in German Samoa." *New Zealand Journal of History*, 11 (October 1977), 155-79.

Saudi Arabia

1184. Knight, G. R. *Report to the government of the Kingdom of Saudi Arabia on manpower assessment and planning.* Geneva: I.L.O., 1972. iii, 48p.

1185. Francis, O. J. C. *Saudi Arabia: manpower planning.* Geneva: I.L.O., 1975. 21p.

1186. Gadi, A. A. *Utilization of human resources: the case of women in Saudi Arabia.* Sacramento: California State University, 1979. xiv, 134p.

1187. Choudhury, M. A. *Manpower planning and policies for Saudi Arabia.* St. John: Memorial University of Newfoundland Press, 1982. ix, 84p.

Senegal

1188. Gery, C. "Underemployment, petty production and government promotion schemes in Senegal." *I.D.S. Bulletin*, 9, 3 (February 1978), 11-16.

1189. Derrien, J. M. *Conditions de travail et sous-développement: les industries agro-alimentaires au Senegal et au Togo.* Paris: C.N.R.S., 296p.

1190. International Labour Organisation. Jobs and Skills Programme for Africa. *Problèmes d'emploi et de formation lies au programme de l'organisation pour la mise en valeur du fleuve Senegal.* Addis Ababa: I.L.O., 1981. 127p.

1191. Martens, G. R. *Industrial relations and the political process in Senegal.* Geneva: International Institute for Labour Studies, 1982. viii, 122p.

1192. Martens, G. R. *Relations professionnelles de l'évolution politique* *au Senegal.* Geneva: International Institute for Labour Studies, 1983. viii, 149p.

See also 23, 28, 100, 107.

Sierra Leone

1193. Yadi, M. *Employment promotion problems in the economic and social development of Sierra Leone.* Geneva: International Institute for Labour Studies, 1972. 66p.

1194. Ketkar, S. L. "Manpower planning for economic development in Sierra Leone." *Manpower and Unemployment Research in Africa: a Newsletter,* 8, 1 (April 1975), 27-44.

1195. International Labour Organisation. Jobs and Skills Programme for Africa. *Ensuring equitable growth: a strategy for increasing employment, equity and basic needs satisfaction in Sierra Leone.* Addis Ababa: I.L.O., 1981. xxxv, 313p.

1196. Stevens, Y. *Technologies for rural women's activities: problems and prospects in Sierra Leone.* Geneva: I.L.O., 1981. ii, 82p.

1197. International Labour Organisation. *Report of the National Tripartite Seminar on the Development of Labour Relations in Sierra Leone, Freetown, 1982.* Geneva: I.L.O., 1982. 8p.

1198. International Labour Organisation. *Republic of Sierra Leone: vocational training programmes.* Geneva: I.L.O., 1982. ii, 27p.

See also 12, 135, 148.

Singapore

1199. National Trades Union Congress. *Why labour must go modern.* Singapore: N.T.U.C., 1970. 282p.

   NTUC case for a non-confrontational labour movement.

1200. Tan, Boon Chiang. "The role of labour law in Singapore." International Labour Organisation. *The role of labour law in developing countries.* Geneva: I.L.O., 1975. p.186-201. (Labour-management relations series, 49).

1201. Kassalow. Everett M. "Aspects of labour relations in multinational companies: an overview of three Asian countries." *International*

Labour Review, 117, 3 (May-June 1978), 273-87.

1202. Ow, Chin Hock and Tyabji, Amina. "Labour-management relations in public enterprises: the case in Singapore." Wehmhoerner, Arnold (ed.) *Labour-management relations in public enterprises in Asia.* Bangkok: Friedrich-Ebert-Stiftung, 1978. p.293-320.

1203. Pang, Eng Fong and Cheng, Leonard. "Changing patterns of industrial relations in Singapore." Kassalow, Everett M. and Damachi, Ukandi G. (eds.) *The role of trade unions in developing societies.* Geneva: International Institute for Labour Studies, 1978. p.124-33.

1204. Lee, Boon Hiok. *Public sector labour relations in the Singapore context.* Singapore: National University of Singapore, Department of Political Science, 1979. (Occasional paper 37).

1205. Tan, Boon Chiang. "Industrial conflict and resolution: the Singapore experience." *Proceedings of Asian Regional Conference on Industrial Relations.* Tokyo: Japan Institute of Labour, 1979. p.197-209.

1206. Levine, Solomon B. "Changing strategies of unions and management: evaluation of four industrialised countries." *British Journal of Industrial Relations*, 18, 1 (March 1980), 70-81.

1207. Deyo, Frederick. *Dependent development and industrial order: an Asian case study.* New York: Praeger, 1981. 138p.

Government incorporation of trade unions in Singapore.

1208. Pang, Eng Fong. "Singapore." Blum, Albert, (ed.) *International handbook of industrial relations: contemporary developments and research.* Westport: Greenwood Press, 1981. p.481-97.

1209. Devan Nair, C.V. *Not by wages alone.* Singapore: Federal, 1982. 413p.

Speeches and articles of the former Singapore NTUC leader responsible for the incorporation of the labour movement which constitute an ideology of Singapore's industrial relations.

1210. Tan, Boon Chiang. "Labour relations and development in Singapore." International Labour Organisation. *Labour relations and development: country studies on Japan, the Philippines, Singapore and Sri Lanka.* Geneva: I.L.O., 1982. p.55-104. (Labour-management relations series, 59).

1211. Leggett, Chris, Wong, Evelyn and Ariff, Mohamed. "Technological change and industrial relations in Singapore." Bamber, Greg and

Lansbury, Russell (eds.) *Bulletin of Comparative Labour Relations*, 12 (1983), 55-75.

1212. Pang, Eng Fong. *Wage policy in Singapore: recent developments and prospects*. Singapore: Economic Research Centre, 1983. 36p.

1213. Wong, Evelyn. "Industrial relations in Singapore: challenge for the 1980s." Institute of Southeast Asian Studies. *Southeast Asian Affairs 1983*. Aldershot: Gower, 1983. p.264-73.

1214. Anantaraman, Venkatraman. "Significance of non-adversative union-management relations in Singapore." *Singapore Management Review*, 6, 1 (January 1984), 35-48.

1215. Krislov, Joseph and Leggett, Chris. "The impact of Singapore's "congenial" labour relations ethic on the conciliation service." *Singapore Management Review*, 6, 2 (July 1984), 95-104.

1216. Leggett, Chris. "Airline pilots and public industrial relations: the case of Singapore Airlines." *Indian Journal of Industrial Relations*, 20, 1 (July 1984), 27-43.

Organised industrial action in a non-confrontational industrial relations climate.

1217. Lim, Linda and Pang, Eng Fong. "Labour strategies and the high-tech challenge: the case of Singapore." *Euro-Asia Business Review*, 3, 2 (April 1984), 27-31.

1218. Murugasu, Sheila. *Handbook of Singapore employment law*. Singapore: Butterworths, 1984. 749p.

See also 3, 55, 90, 134, 153, 158.

South Africa

1219. South African Institute of Race Relations. *Surveys of Race Relations*. Johannesburg: The Institute, annual. 1946-

Includes developments in employment and labour matters.

1220. United States. Bureau of Labor Statistics. *Labour law and practice in South Africa*. Washington: U.S.G.P.O., 1962. 44p.

1221. International Labour Office. *Special reports of the Director-General on the application of the declaration concerning the policy of apartheid of the Republic of South Africa*. Geneva: I.L.O., 1965-.

1222. Wilson, Francis A. H. *Migrant labour in South Africa.* Johannesburg: South African Council of Churches (SPRO-CAS), 1972. 281p.

1223. Rex, John. "The plural society: the South African case." Leftwick, Adrian (ed.) *South African economic growth and political change.* London: Allison & Busby, 1974.

1224. Thomas, Wolfgang (ed.) *Labour perspectives on South Africa.* Cape Town: David Philip, 1974. 259p.

1225. Douwes Dekker, Loet. "Case studies in African labour action." Sandbrook, Richard and Cohen, Robin (eds.) *The development of an African working class.* London: Longman, 1975. p.207-38.

1226. Schlemmer, Laurie and Webster, Eddie. *Change, reform and economic growth.* Johannesburg: Raven Press, 1977.

1227. Simpkins, C. E. W. and Clark, D. G. (eds.) *Structural unemployment in South Africa.* Durban: Natal University Press, 1978.

1228. Jowell, Kate. "Labour policy in South Africa." *South African Journal of Economics,* 47, 4 (1979), 386-96.

1229. Jubber, Ken (ed.) *Industrial relations and industrial sociology.* Cape Town: Juta, 1979. 260p.

1230. Savage, Mike. "The ownership and control of large South African companies." Jubber, Ken (ed.) *op cit* p.36-62.

1231. Thomas, Wolfgang. "The socio-political structure of the South African economy." Jubber, Ken (ed.) *op cit* p.1-35.

1232. Van Coller, Sam. "A framework for developing a management strategy in industrial relations." Jubber, Ken (ed.) *op cit* p.98-126.

1233. Williams, Kelvin. "Trade unionism in South African history." Jubber, Ken (ed.) *op cit* p.63-83.

1234. Greenberg, Sidney B. *Race and state in capitalist development: South Africa in comparative perspective.* Johannesburg: Raven Press, 1980.

1235. Luckhardt, Ken and Wall, Brenda. *Organise ... or starve! The history of the South African Congress of Trade Unions.* London: Lawrence & Wishart, 1980. 520p.

1236. Department of Manpower. *Reports of the National Manpower Commission.* Pretoria: Republic of South Africa, 1981-.

1237. Du Toit, Darcy. *Capital and labour in South Africa: class* *struggles in the 1970s.* London: Kegan Paul, 1981. 495p.

1238. Kane Berman, John. "The challenge of black unions." *South African Journal of Labour Relations*, 5, 2 (1981), 28-39.

1239. Hauck, David. *Black trade unions in South Africa.* Washington: Investor Responsibility Research Center, 1982.

1240. Miller, Shirley. *Trade unions in South Africa 1970-1980: a directory and statistics.* Cape Town: University of Cape Town, Southern Africa Labour and Development Research Unit, 1982. 278p. (SALDRU working paper 45).

1241. Van Der Merwe, Roux. "Trade unions and the democratic order." *Optima*, 31, 4 (1983), 160-9.

Spain

1242. Witney, Fred. *Labor policy and practices in Spain: a study of employer-employee relations under the Franco regime.* New York: Praeger, 1965. 103p.

1243. Martinez-Alier, Juan. *Labourers and landowners in southern Spain.* London: Allen & Unwin, 1971. 352p.

1244. Maravall, Casenoves H. "Politica de empleo: una rama del derecho del trabajo." *Revista de Trabajo*, 35-36 (July-December 1971), 5-36.

1245. Amsden, Jon. *Collective bargaining and class conflict in Spain.* London: Weidenfeld & Nicolson, 1972. 204p.

1246. Garrido, Falla F. "Constitutional background and implications of the new Spanish Trade Union Act." *International Labour Review*, 105, 3 (March 1972), 261-73.

1247. Martin, Villa R. "Spanish Trade Union Act and the I.L.O. constitution." *International Labour Review*, 105, 3 (March 1972), 275-93.

1248. Ruiz-Jimenez, Carlos J. "Reflections on the new Spanish Trade Union Act." *International Labour Review*, 105, 3 (March 1972), 205-40.

1249. Tiemo, Galvan E. "Some comments on the Spanish Trade Union Act of 17 February 1971." *International Labour Review*, 105, 3 (March 1972), 245-60.

1250. Tunon de Lara, M. *Movimiento obrero en la historia de España.* Madrid: Taurus, 1972. 963p.

1251. Garcia, Barbanoho A. "Crecimiento economico y la evolucion del empleo." *Revista de Estudios Agro-Sociales,* 22, 84 (July-September 1973), 127-44.

1252. Spain. Ministero de Trabajo. *Empleo: decreto 3090/1972 y disposiciones para su desarrollo.* Madrid: Ministero, 1973. 84p.

1253. Cercos, Perez A. "Empleo en el sector agrario." *Revista de Estudios Agro-Sociales,* 23, 86 (January-March 1974), 7-22.

1254. Data S.A. (Madrid) *Fringe benefits: a survey of private companies.* Second edition. Madrid: Data S.A., 1974. 117p.

1255. Horowitz, Morris A. *Manpower and education in Franco Spain.* Hamden, Conn.: Shoe String Press, 1974. 164p.

1256. Rodriguez, Nuno V. "Analisis regional de la poblacion activa Española en el periodo 1962-1971." *De Economia,* 28, 132 (January-March 1975), 93-157.

1257. Camacho, M. *Ecrits de la prison: le mouvement syndical espagnol et les commissions ouvrières.* Paris: Editions Sociales, 1976. 155p.

1258. Sana, H. *Syndicalismo y autogestion.* Madrid: G. del Taro, 1977. 239p.

1259. Maravall, Jose. *Dictatorship and political dissent: workers and students in Franco's Spain.* London: Tavistock, 1978. 199p.

1260. Eaton, Jack. "The Basque workers' co-operatives." *Industrial Relations Journal,* 10, 3 (Autumn 1979), 32-40.

1261. Serano, A. and Malo de Molina, J. L. *Salarios y mercado de trabajo en España.* Madrid: H. Blume Ediciones, 1979. 365p.

1262. Ojeda, Aviles A. *Derecho syndical.* Madrid: Editorial Technos, 1980. 504p.

1263. Industrial Relations Services. "Spain: a changing framework for industrial action." *European Industrial Relations Review,* 95 (December 1981), 12-14.

1264. Industrial Relations Services. "Spain: negotiating on productivity and absenteeism." *European Industrial Relations Review,* 88 (May 1981), 5-6.

1265. Industrial Relations Services. "Spain: new employment contract laws." *European Industrial Relations Review,* 92 (September 1981), 8-9.

1266. Industrial Relations Services. "Spain: social contract analysis."

European Industrial Relations Review, 91 (August 1981), 5-6.

1267. Sagardoy Bengoechea, J. A. "Spanish workers' statute." *International Labour Review*, 120, 2 (March-April 1981), 215-29.

1268. Union General de Trabajadores de España. *Acuerdo nacional sobre empleo.* Madrid: U.G.T.E., 1981. 301p.

1269. Industrial Relations Services. "Spain: bargaining under a social contract." *European Industrial relations Review*, 102 (July 1982), 12-14.

1270. Industrial Relations Services. "Spain: temporary work and job creation." *European Industrial Relations Review*, 104 (September 1982), 16-19.

1271. Thomas, H. and Logan, C. *Mondragon: an economic analysis.* London: Allen& Unwin, 1982. viii, 218p.

1272. Winston, Colin M. "The proletarian carlist road to fascism: Sindicalismo Libre." *Journal of Contemporary History*, 17 (October 1982), 557-85.

1273. Confederacion Española de Organizaciones Empresariales. *Prevencion de riesgos professionales.* Madrid: C.E.O.E., 1983. 366p.

1274. Cusas Baamonde, M. E. "Representacion unitaria de los trabajadores en la empresa y negociacion colectiva." *Civitas*, 13 (January-March 1983), 15-62.

1275. Gonzalez Gavira, A. J. and Gregaria de Tejada, J. M. "Termino representantes de los trabajadores en la incoacion de procedimiento de conflicto colectivo." *Civitas*, 14 (April-June 1983), 277-91.

1276. Industrial Relations Services. "Spain: towards a new form of bargaining framework." *European Industrial Relations Review*, 116 (September 1983), 13-14.

1277. Industrial Relations Services. "Spain: the working time controversy." *European Industrial Relations Review*, 118 (November 1983), 9-10.

1278. Malo de Molina, J. L. *Rigidez o flexibilidad del mercado de trabajo? La experiencia Español durante la crisis.* Madrid: Banco de España, 1983. 63p.

1279. Ojeda, Aviles A. "Procedimiento de colacacion revisitado." *Civitas*, 14 (April-June 1983), 203-34.

1280. Fina, I. and Hawkesworth, R. I. "Trade unions and collective bargaining in post-Franco Spain." *Labour and Society*, 9, 1 (January-March 1984), 3-27.

See also 14, 96, 132.

Sri Lanka

1281. Jankaric, I. *Employment and unemployment with specific reflex on tertiary sector (study case Ceylon).* The Hague: Institute of Social Studies, 1968. 28p.

1282. Ceylon. Official Committee on the Problem of Unemployment amongst Graduates. *Report of the ... Committee...* Colombo: The Committee, 1969. 46p.

1283. Seers, D. "New light on structural unemployment: lessons of a mission to Ceylon." *Pakistan Labour Gazette*, 18, 4 (October-December 1970), 381-9.

1284. Srivastava, R. K. *Unemployment, employment policy and employment targets.* Geneva: International Institute for Labour Studies, 1970. 19p.

1285. International Labour Organisation. *Matching employment opportunities and expectations: a programme of action for Ceylon.* Geneva: I.L.O., 1971. Two volumes. 251p., 251p.

1286. Jones, G. W. and Selvaratnam, S. "Some problems of employment creation in Ceylon." *Marga*, 1, 1 (1971), 72-91.

1287. Kearney, R. N. *Trade unions and politics in Ceylon.* Berkeley: University of California Press, 1971. xv, 195p.

1288. Richards, P. J. *Employment and unemployment in Ceylon.* Paris: O.E.C.D., 1971. 211p.

1289. Richards, P. J. "Unemployment in Ceylon: the figures and the facts." *Marga*, 1, 2 (1971), 83-92.

1290. Srivastava, R. K. and Selvaratnam, S. *Employment situation and trends.* Colombo: I.L.O., 1971. 134p.

1291. Sugathapala, T. O. *Some aspects of disciplinary proceedings in the public service of Ceylon.* Colombo: Academy of Administrative Studies, 1971. 40p.

1292. Ceylon. Department of Labour. *May Day 1972.* Colombo: The Department, 1972. 80p.

Collection of articles on labour matters.

1293. De Mel, W. L. P. "Evolution of industrial relations in Ceylon." *Ceylon Labour Gazette*, 23, 4 (April 1972), 229-50; 23, 5 (May 1972), 307-20.

1294. De Mel, L. *Evolution of industrial relations in Ceylon: with special reference to plantations.* Geneva: International Institute for Labour Studies, 1972. 27p.

1295. Jayawardena, V. K. *Rise of the labor movement in Ceylon.* Durham, N.C.: Duke University Press, 1972. xvi, 382p.

1296. Moller, Birger. *Employment approaches to economic planning in developing countries, with special reference to ... Ceylon.* Lund: Studentlitteratur, 1972. 305p.

1297. Rasaratnam, C. T. "Collective bargaining in Ceylon." *Ceylon Labour Gazette*, 23, 1 (January 1972), 3-12; 23, 2 (February 1972), 105-16.

1298. Seers, D. "New light on structural unemployment: lessons of a mission to Ceylon." *International Labour Review*, 105, 2 (February 1972), 99-108.

1299. Srivastava, R. K. and Selvaratnam, S. "Youth employment in Ceylon." *Marga*, 1, 4 (1972), 27-59.

1300. International Labour Organisation. *Employment policy in the 2nd development decade: a U.N. family approach.* Geneva: I.L.O., 1973. viii, 44p.

1301. Richards, P. J. "Job mobility and unemployment in the Ceylon urban labour market." *Oxford Bulletin of Economics and Statistics*, 35, 1 (February 1973), 49-59.

1302. Sooriarachchi, S. W. "Industrial relations and development in Ceylon." *Sri Lanka Labour Gazette*, 23, 12 (December 1982), 785-96; 24, 1 (January 1973), 3-13.

1303. Sri Lanka. Department of Labour. Library. *Subject index to the Industrial Court awards.* Colombo: The Department, 1973. xli, 148p.

1304. Srivastava, R. K. "Unemployment problem with special reference to the private sector." *Marga*, 2, 2 (1973), 49-60.

1305. Appadurai, E. S. *Industrial relations in Sri Lanka and the role of the Employers' Federation of Ceylon.* Geneva: I.L.O., 1974. 7p.

1306. De Mel, W. L. P. "Workers' participation in decisions within undertakings in Sri Lanka." *Sri Lanka Labour Gazette*, 25, 12 (December 1974), 781-8.

1307. Rasavatnam, C. T. "Women and employment in Sri Lanka." *Sri Lanka Labour Gazette*, 25, 6 (June 1974), 358-72.

1308. Sri Lanka. Department of Labour. Library. *Subject guide to reported cases on labour law.* Colombo: The Department, 1974. xxxv, 177p.

1309. Srivastava, R. K. *Sri Lanka: employment and human resources planning.* Geneva: I.L.O., 1975. 28p.

1310. Weerasinghe, D. P. A. "Role of government in industrial relations: a comparative study of the industrial relations systems in Great Britain and Sri Lanka." *Sri Lanka Labour Gazette*, 26, 6 (June 1975), 315-22.

1311. Warnapala, W. A. W. "Workers' councils and advisory committees in Sri Lanka." *Indian Journal of Industrial Relations*, 11, 1 (July 1975), 3-16.

1312. International Labour Organisation. *Report of the wage survey in Sri Lanka.* Bangkok: I.L.O., 1976.

1313. Perera, U. L. J. and Gunawardena, P. J. *Study of hired labourers in peasant agriculture in Sri Lanka.* Colombo: Agrarian Research and Training Institute, 1980. vi, 140p.

1314. Karale, S. R. *Bibliography of labour relations in Sri Lanka, 1840-1978.* Colombo: Ministry of Labour, 1981.

1315. Kariyawasan, U. *Industrial relations and the political process in Sri Lanka.* Geneva: International Institute for Labour Studies, 1981. 41p.

1316. Kurian, R. *Position of women workers in the plantation sector in Sri Lanka.* Geneva: I.L.O., 1981. xi, 180p.

1317. National Tripartite Seminar on the Improvement of Working Conditions and Environment in Sri Lanka, Colombo, 1980. *Report of the ... Seminar.* Colombo: I.L.O., 1981. iii, 301p.

1318. Radovanovic, B. and Kavcic, B. "Evaluation of the development of worker participation in Sri Lanka." *Sri Lanka Labour Gazette*, 32, 3 (July-September 1981), 29-35.

1319. Soysa, G. D. G. P. *Worker participation in decisions within the* *undertakings of Sri Lanka.* Geneva: I.L.O., 1981. 2p.

1320. Vijayyasingan, N. *Sri Lanka's experiment on workers' participation in decisions within undertakings.* Geneva: I.L.O., 1981. 4p.

1321. De Silva, S. R. *Disciplinary action and disciplinary procedures in the private sector.* Colombo: Employers' Federation of Ceylon, 1982. 39p.

1322. Perera, S. E. G. *Industrial shift work practices and problems of shift workers in Sri Lanka.* Bangkok: I.L.O., 1982. 33p.

1323. De Silva, S. R. *Contract of Employment.* Colombo: Employers' Federation of Ceylon, 1983. xxi, 224p.

1324. Hallett, A. J. H. "Employment, investment and production in Sri Lanka 1959-80: reflections on what the figures reveal." *Marga,* 7, 1 (1983), 78-100.

1325. Jayawardena, K. "The plantation sector in Sri Lanka: recent changes in the welfare of children and women." *World Development,* 12 (March 1984), 317-28.

See also 1, 23, 27, 82, 105, 133, 134, 153.

Sudan

1326. United Nations. Department of Economic and Social Affairs. *Population growth and manpower in the Sudan.* New York: U.N., 1964. 150p.

1327. Taha, A. *Sudanese labour movement: a study of labour unionism in a developing society.* Los Angeles: University of California, 1970. 259p.

1328. Agabani, S. S. *Industrial relations and economic development: the Sudan case.* The Hague: Institute of Social Studies, 1972. 62p.

1329. Mustafa, M. M. *Manpower and employment problems in the Sudan.* Geneva: International Institute for Labour Studies, 1972. 20p.

1330. Goundrey, G. K. *Report to the government of the Republic of the Sudan on the development and implementation of a national employment policy.* Geneva: I.L.O., 1973. iv, 181p.

1331. Taha, A. R. E. A. and Jack, A. H. "Termination of employment in the Sudan: the search for a compromise." *Bulletin of the International Institute for Labour Studies,* 11 (1973), 35-40.

1332. Kannappan, S. "Urban labour market in Sudan: some implications for current theorising." Industrial Relations Research Association. *Proceedings*, 28, 1975. 9-16.

1333. Mulat, T. *Educated unemployment in the Sudan.* Geneva: I.L.O., 1975. ii, 46p.

1334. Sanyal, B. C. and Versluis, J. *Education and employment research project: higher education, human capital and labour market segmentation in the Sudan.* Geneva: I.L.O., 1976. 42p.

1335. Taha, A. R. E. A. and Jack, A. H. *Role of trade unions and employers' associations in socio-economic development in the Sudan.* Geneva: International Institute for Labour Studies, 1976. 15p.

1336. Suliman, A. A. *Factors affecting public sector salaries policies in the Sudan.* Khartoum: University of Khartoum, 1979. ii, 152p.

1337. International Labour Organisation. *Report of the National Tripartite Seminar on Labour Relations in the Sudan, Khartoum, 1980.* Geneva: I.L.O., 1982. 8p.

1338. Taha, A. R. E. A. "Industrial relations in the Sudan." *Labour and Society*, 7, 2 (April-June 1982), 137-56.

1339. El-Bagir, I., Dey, J., Ghosh, J. and Ali, A. A. G. *Labour markets in Sudan.* Geneva: I.L.O., 1984. vi, 224p.

See also 6, 42, 141.

Swaziland

1340. Cracknell, B. E., Wilson, A. and Stevens, N. *Manpower review: Swaziland 1980.* London: Overseas Development Administration, 1980. 47p.

1341. International Labour Organisation. *Swaziland: development and improvement of workmen's compensation law and administration.* Geneva: I.L.O., 1983. 27p.

1342. Russell, Margo. "Beyond remittances: the redistribution of cash in Swazi society." *Journal of Modern African Studies*, 22, 4 (December 1984), 595-616.

See also 50, 58, 144, 147.

Sweden

1343. Johnston, T. L. *Collective bargaining in Sweden.* London: Allen & Unwin, 1962.

1344. Schmidt, Folke. *The law of labour relations in Sweden.* Harvard University Press, 1962.

1345. Anderman, S. D. (ed.) *Trade unions and technological change.* London: Allen & Unwin, 1967.

1346. Peterson, Richard B. "The Swedish experience with industrial democracy." *British Journal of Industrial Relations.* 6, 2 (July 1968), 185-203.

1347. Fulcher, James. "Discontent in a Swedish shipyard: the Knockums report." *British Journal of Industrial relations*, 11, 2 (July 1973), 242-58.

1348. Jenkins, David. *Job reform in Sweden.* Swedish Employers' Confederation, 1975.

1349. Dahlstrom, E. *Efficiency, satisfaction and democracy in work: ideas of industrial relations in post-war Sweden.* Gothenburg: Sociologiska Institutionen, 1976.

1350. Jackson, Peter. "Employers' confederations in Sweden and the UK and the significance of industrial infrastructure." *British Journal of Industrial Relations*, 14, 3 (November 1976), 306-23.

1351. Schmidt, Folke. *Law and industrial relations in Sweden.* Rothman, 1977.

1352. Korpi, Walter. *The working class in welfare capitalism.* London: Routledge & Kegan Paul, 1978.

1353. Korpi, Walter. "Workplace bargaining, the law and unofficial strikes: the case of Sweden." *British Journal of Industrial Relations*, 16, 3 (November 1978), 355-68.

1354. Myrdal, H. G. "The Swedish model: will it survive?" *British Journal of Industrial Relations*, 18, 1 (March 1980), 57-69.

1355. Jones, H. G. "The Swedish industrial scene." *Journal of Industrial Affairs*, 8 (Spring 1981), 35-9.

1356. Korpi, Walter. "Unofficial strikes in Sweden." *British Journal of Industrial Relations*, 19, 1 (March 1981), 66-86.

1357. Calmfors, L. and Viotti, S. "Wage indexation, the Scandinavian model and macroeconomic stability in the open economy." *Oxford Economic Papers*, 34 (November 1982), 546-66.

1358. Prais, S. J. "Strike frequencies and plant size: a comment on Swedish and U.K. experience." *British Journal of Industrial Relations*, 20, 1 (March 1982), 101-4.

See also 13, 37, 40, 95, 99, 154.

Switzerland

1359. Groupe de Travail pour l'Histoire du Mouvement Ouvrier en Suisse. *Bibliographie du mouvement ouvrier suisse*. Lausanne: Le Groupe, 1968-71. Three volumes.

1360. Thalmann-Antenen, H. "Equal pay: the position in Switzerland." *International Labour Review*, 104, 4 (October 1971), 275-88.

1361. Willatt, N. "Flextime at Sandoz." *European Business*, 34 (Autumn 1973), 56-61.

1362. Willatt, N. "Why Switzerland works." *Management Today*, (May 1974), 56-9.

1363. Allenspack, H. *Flexible working hours*. Geneva: I.L.O., 1975. v, 64p.

1364. Groupe de Travail pour l'Histoire du Mouvement Ouvrier en Suisse. *Mouvement ouvrier suisse, documents: situation, organisation et luttes de travailleurs de 1800 á nos jours*. Geneva: Editions Adversaires, 1975. 420p.

1365. Zentralverband Schweizerischer Arbeitgeberorganisationen. "Occupation et marché de l'emploi." *Journal des Associations Patronales*, 70, 14 (3 April 1975), 235-7.

1366. Industrial Relations Services. "Switzerland: industrial relations in context." *European Industrial Relations Review*, 72, (January 1980), 16-18; 81 (October 1980), 15-16.

1367. Blattner, N. *Review of selected national reports on the employment impact of microelectronics*. Basel: Basel Universitaet, Institut fuer Angewandte Wirtschaftsforschung, 1981. 38p.

1368. Höpflinger, F. "White collar unions in Switzerland." *Industrial Relations Journal*, 12, 4 (July-August 1981), 58-64.

1369. Berenstein, A. *Contrat de travail: un siècle d'évolution legislative*.

Fribourg: Universitaetsverlag Freiburg Schweiz, 1982. 29p.

1370. Switzerland. Office Federal de l'Industrie, des Arts et Metiers et du Travail. *Formes particulières de l'amenagement du temps de travail.* Berne: l'Office, 1982. v, 60p.

1371. Vischer, F. *Contrat de travail.* Fribourg: Editions Universitaires, 1982. 255p.

1372. Maillat, D. *Fonctionnement du marché de l'emploi au niveau local.* Saint-Sapharin: Editions Georgi, 1983. 187p.

1373. Dreifuss, R. "Vers la semaine de quarante heures." *Vie Economique*, 57, 4 (April 1984), 181.

See also 151.

Syria

1374. Hamoudi, Q. *Applications des conventions et récommendations internationales du travail par les états arabes.* Lille: Université de Lille, 1974. iv, 321p.

1375. International Labour Organisation. *Technical memorandum to the government of the Syrian Arab Republic on conditions of employment and administration of shipboard personnel.* Geneva: I.L.O., 1982. 24p.

See also 25.

Tanzania

1376. Ray, R. S. *Labour force survey of Tanzania*. Dar-es-Salaam: Ministry of Economic Affairs, 1966. x, 156p.

1377. Mapolu, H. *Organisation and participation of workers in Tanzania*. Dar-es-Salaam: [n.p.], 1972. 43p.

1378. Okulo, H. A. "Manpower development in Tanzania." *Bulletin of the International Institute for Labour Studies*, 9 (1972), 75-90.

1379 Bienefeld, M. A. *Self-employed of urban Tanzania*. Brighton: University of Sussex: Institute of Development Studies, 1974. 53p.

1380. Mihyo, P. "Struggle for workers' control in Tanzania." *Review of African Political Economy*, 4 (November 1975), 62-84.

1381. Mapolu, Henry (ed.) *Workers and management*. Dar-es-Salaam: Tanzania Publishing House, 1976. 257p.

1382. Khamis, I. A. *Labour economics and manpower planning in Tanzania*. Nairobi: Kenya Literary Bureau, 1978. 141p.

1383. Bienefeld, M. "Trade unions, the labour process and the Tanzanian state." *Journal of Modern African Studies*, 17 (December 1979), 553-93.

1384. Jackson, Dudley. "The disappearance of strikes in Tanzania." *Journal of Modern African Studies*, 17 (June 1979), 219-51.

1385. Mapolu, H. *Workers' participation in the management of public enterprise*. Dakar: Council for the Development of Economic and Social Research in Africa, 1980. 19p.

1386. International Labour Organisation. *United Republic of Tanzania: manpower and employment planning*. Geneva: I.L.O., 1982. 35p.

1387. Knight, J. B. and Sabot, R. H. "From migrants to proletarians: employment experience, mobility and wages in Tanzania." *Oxford Bulletin of Economics and Statistics*, 44, 3 (August 1982), 199-226.

1388. Knight, J. B. and Sabot, R. H. "Role of the firm in wage determination: an African case study." *Oxford Economic Papers*, 35, 1 (March 1983), 45-66.

1389. Lindauer, D. I. and Sabot, R. H. "Public/private wage differential in an urban economy." *Journal of Development Economics*, 12, 1-2 (February-April 1983), 137-52.

1390. Leonor, M. D. *Basic needs and employment: unemployment and* *the education system in Tanzania.* Geneva: I.L.O., 1983. 46p.

See also 19, 87, 105, 106, 110, 111, 112, 141.

Thailand

1391. Chamnong, Vudhichai. *Industrial relations and development in Thailand.* Bangkok: I.L.O., 1979. 83p.

1392. Chamnong, Vudhichai. *Industrial relations and development in Thailand: a study prepared for the ILO.* Bangkok: I.L.O., 1979. 59p.

1393. Chanda, S. "Collective bargaining and labour arbitration." Wehmhoerner, Arnold (ed.) *South Asia.* Bangkok, 1979.

1394. Manusphaibool, Supachai. "Industrial conflict and resolution: Thailand." Asian Regional Conference on Industrial Relations. *Proceedings.* Tokyo: Japan Institute of Labour, 1979. p.133-44.

1395. Phipatanakul, Phaisith. "Industrial democracy in Thailand." Wehmhoerner, Arnold (ed.) *Industrial democracy in Asia.* Bangkok: Friedrich-Ebert-Stiftung, 1980. p.359-70.

1396. Rabibhadana, Akin. "Patron-client relationships and self-help organisations of the poor." Paper presented at the Thai-European Seminar on Social Change in Contemporary Thailand. Amsterdam: [n.p.], 1980.

1397. Schregle, Johannes."Keynote address." Wehmhoerner, Arnold (ed.) *Industrial democracy in Asia.* Bangkok: Friedrich-Ebert-Stiftung, 1980.

1398. Chandravithun, Nikom. *Thai labour: a long journey.* Bangkok: Thai Watana Panich Co. Ltd., 1982. 165p.

1399. Hongladarom, Chira (ed.) *Comparative labour and management.* Pataya: Thamsat University Press, 1982. 151p.

1400. Hongladarom, Chira and Chongsiriwatana, Wanee. *Case studies on labor relations at the level of the enterprise in Asia.* Pataya: Thamasat University, Human Resource Institute, 1982. 106p.

1401. Wehmhoerner, Arnold. "Trade unionism in Thailand: a new dimension in a modernising society." *Journal of Contemporary Asia*, 13, 4 (1983), 481-97.

1402. Harriman, Ed. "Nothing to do with us: British companies' involvement in Bangkok sweatshops." *New Statesman*, (9 March 1984),

19-20.

1403. Marsden, K. "Services for small firms: the role of government programmes and market networks in Thailand." *International Labour Review*, 123, 2 (March-April 1984), 235-50.

See also 133.

Togo

1404. Lobstein, P. and Irani, H. *Togo: Possibilités d'emploi des methodes á fort coefficient de main-d'oeuvre.* Geneva: I.L.O., 1975. ii, 80p.

1405. Natchaba, C. F. "Unité du syndicalisme Togolais." *Penant*, 92 (July-December 1982), 32-72.

1406. International Labour Organisation. Jobs and Skills Programme for Africa. *Eléments pour une stratégie d'emploi dans les zones rurales au Togo.* Addis Ababa: I.L.O., 1983. 79p.

See also 100, 109.

Tunisia

1407. Beling, Willard A. *Modernization and African labour: a Tunisian case study.* New York: Praeger, 1965. 259p.

1408. Carter, Florence. *Labor law and practice in Tunisia.* Washington: U.S.G.P.O., 1965. 68p.

1409. Rabah, T. and B'Chir, B. "Formes de motivation et productivité dans une entreprise tunisienne de service." *Revue Africaine de Management*, 1, 2 (1972), 103-36.

1410. Tunisia. Ministère du Plan. *Situation de l'emploi dans le gouvernement de Kairouan.* Tunis: La Ministère, 1973. 133p.

1411. Tunisia. Ministère du Plan. *Situation de l'emploi dans la gouvernement de Kasserine.* Tunis: La Ministère, 1973. 159p.

1412. International Labour Organisation. *Tunisie: évaluation et planification de l'emploi.* Geneva: I.L.O., 1974. ii, 144p.

1413. Clemenceau, P. and Hadjadj, B. *Contribution á l'analyse des problèmes d'emploi et de formation en Tunisie.* Tunis: Ministère du Plan, 1976. Two volumes.

1414. Ahmed, E. and Schaar, S. "M'hamed Ali and the Tunisian labour movement." *Race and Class,* 19 (Winter 1978), 253-76.

1415. Liauzu, C. *Salariat et mouvement ouvrier en Tunisie: crises et mutations, 1931-1939.* Paris: Editions du Centre National de la Récherche Scientifique, 1978. 192p.

1416. Merson, B. *Country labour profile: Tunisia.* Washington: U.S.G.P.O., 1980. 6p.

1417. Taamallah, K. "Evolution de l'emploi en Tunisie." *Revue Tunisienne de Sciences Sociales,* 17, 60 (1980), 17-55.

1418. Ben Abdallah, E. H. *Participation des travailleurs aux décisions dans l'entreprise en Tunisie.* Geneva: I.L.O., 1981. 26p.

1419. Esseghir, A. *Conciliation en Tunisie.* Geneva: I.L.O., 1981. 16p.

1420. International Labour Organisation. *Memorandum au gouvernement de la Tunisie sur la politique des salaires et les classifications professionnelles.* Geneva: I.L.O., 1982. 24p.

1421. Belaid, H. "Implantation syndicale en milieu rural au Magreb." *U Travail et Développement,* 1 (January-June 1983), 9-31.

See also 109.

Turkey

1422. International Labour Organisation. *Report to the government of Turkey on the visit of a joint mission of experts on labour-management relations.* Geneva: I.L.O., 1963. 70p.

1423. Robinson, Richard D. *High-level manpower in economic development: the Turkish case.* Harvard: Harvard University, Center for Middle Eastern Studies, 134p.

1424. TURK-IS. *Turkish trade union movement.* Ankara: TURK-IS, [197-?]. 68p.

1425. Jackson, Dudley. "The political economy of collective bargaining: the case of Turkey." *British Journal of Industrial Relations,* 9, 1(March 1971), 117-9.

1426. Toruner, M. *Employment and manpower trends in Turkey, 1967-1971.* Ankara: Devlet Planlana Teskilati, 1971. 18p.

1427. Hic, M. *Employment and wages in the automotive and other* *assembly industries in Turkey.* Istanbul: Istanbul University, Iktisat Fakultesi, 1974. 58p.

1428. Paine, Suzanne. *Exporting workers: the Turkish case.* Cambridge: Cambridge University Press, 1974. 227p.

1429. Miller, D. R. *Dynamics of human resources development in Turkey and their implications for employment and income distribution.* Geneva: I.L.O., 1975. 50p.

1430. Roy, Delwin A. "Labour and trade unionism in Turkey: the Eregli coalmines." *Middle Eastern Studies*, 12 (October 1976), 125-72.

1431. Ekin, N. *Development of industrial relations in the mixed economic system of Turkey.* Istanbul: [n.p.], 1979. 61p.

1432. Ekin, N. *Economic and social factors affecting industrial relations in Turkey.* Istanbul: [n.p.], 1979. 35p.

1433. Citci, O. "Women in the Turkish public service." *Turkish Public Administration Annual*, 6-7 (1979-80), 27-53.

1434. Dereli, T. and Ekin, N. *Development of industrial relations in Turkey.* Istanbul: Fatih Yayinevi Matbaasi, 1980. 35p.

1435. Gulmez, M. "Process of interaction and osmosis between systems of labour relations." *Turkish Public Administration Annual*, 6-7 (1979-80), 55-93.

1436. Kandiyoti, D. "Characteristics of the industrial workers in the Istanbul-Izmit complex." *Turkish Public Administration Annual*, 6-7 (1979-80), 135-58.

1437. Elbir, H. K. *Workers' participation in the management of the undertaking under Turkish law.* Geneva: I.L.O., 1981. 7p.

1438. Hodsdon, D. F. *The Turkish Forestry, Land Irrigation, Agriculture and Agricultural Industry Workers' Union.* Geneva: I.L.O., 1981. 46p.

In Turkish. English summary available.

1439. International Labour Organisation. *Technical memorandum to the government of Turkey on procedures for the settlement of labour disputes.* Geneva: I.L.O., 1981. 12p.

1440. Mehmet, O. "Assessment of manpower and educational planning in Turkey: shifting from long-range forecasting to employment policy." *International Journal of Manpower*, 2, 2 (1981), 26-32.

1441. Lagergren, I. *Report on direct contacts mission to Turkey.* Geneva: I.L.O., 1982. 32p.

1442. Turkey. Devlet Istatistik Enstitusu. *Collective bargaining/bargaining agreement statistics.* Ankara: D.I.E., 1982. vii, 20p.

1443. International Labour Organisation. *Republic of Turkey: safety and health in coal mines.* Geneva: I.L.O., 1983. 17p.

1444. Keyder, C. *Social structure and the labour market in Turkish agriculture.* Geneva: I.L.O., 1983. iii, 53p.

See also 35.

Uganda

1445. Scott, Roger. *The development of trade unions in Uganda.* Nairobi: East African Publishing House, 1966. 200p.

1446. Uganda. Ministry of Planning and Economic Development. *High level manpower survey 1967 and analysis of requirements 1967-1981.* The Ministry, 1969. ii, 53p.

1447. Weeks, J. F. "Wage policy and the colonial legacy: a comparative study." *Journal of Modern African Studies,* 5, 3 (October 1971), 361-87.

1448. Hutton, Caroline. *Reluctant farmers? A study of unemployment and planned rural development in Uganda.* Kampala: East African Publishing House, 1973. 330p.

See also 6, 87.

USSR

1449. Dewar, Margaret. *Labour policy in the USSR, 1917-1928.* London: Royal Institute of International Affairs, 1956. 286p.

1450. Roberts, Benjamin Charles and Feingold, Maria. *Trade unions and industrial relations in the Soviet Union.* London: Workers' Educational Association, 1958. 31p.

1451. Osipov, G. V. (ed.) *Industry and labour in the USSR.* London: Tavistock, 1966.

1452. McAuley, Mary. *Labour disputes in Soviet Russia, 1957-1965.* Oxford: Clarendon Press, 1969. 269p.

1453. Dominguez, John R. "An analysis of the industrial relations system in a collective society." *British Journal of Industrial Relations,* 9, 1 (March 1971), 21-32.

1454. Borisova, Y. S. *Outline history of the Soviet working class.* Moscow: Progress, 1973. 387p.

1455. Levine, Irving R. *The new worker in Soviet Russia.* London: Macmillan, 1973. 191p.

1456. Medvedev, Fedor and Kulikov, Gennady. *Soviet trade unions: yesterday, today, tomorrow.* Moscow: All-Union Central Council of Trade Unions, 1976. 191p.

1457. Ellman, Michael. "On a mistake by Preobrazhensky and Stalin." *Journal of Development Studies,* 14 (April 1978), 353-6.

1458. Lane, David and O'Dell, Felicity. *The Soviet industrial worker: social class, education and control.* Oxford: Martin Robertson, 1978. 167p.

1459. Teckenberg, W. "Labour turnover and job satisfaction: indications of industrial conflict in the USSR." *Soviet Studies,* 30 (April 1978), 193-211.

1460. Ruble, B. "Dual functioning trade unions in the USSR." *British Journal of Industrial Relations,* 17, 2 (July 1979), 235-41.

1461. Haynes Viktor and Semyonova, Olga (eds.) *Workers against the Gulag: the new opposition in the Soviet Union.* London: Pluto Press, 1979. 129p.

1462. Kahan, A and Ruble, B. A. (eds.) *Industrial labor in the USSR: [papers of a conference].* London: Pergamon, 1979. 421p.

1463. Adam, Jan. "The present Soviet incentive system." *Soviet Studies,* 32 (July 1980), 349-65.

1464. Nove, Alec. "The labour market in the Soviet Union." *New Society,* (10 April 1980), 58-9.

1465. Ruble, Blair A. *Soviet trade unions: their development in the 1970s.* Cambridge: Cambridge University Press, 1981. 190p.

1466. Schapiro, Leonard and Godson, Joseph (eds.) *The Soviet worker: illusions and realities.* London: Macmillan, 1981. 291p.

1467. Swain, G. R. "Bolsheviks and metal workers on the eve of the First World War." *Journal of Contemporary History,* 16 (April 1981), 273-91.

1468. Adam, Jan (ed.) *Employment policies in the Soviet Union and Eastern Europe.* London: St. Martin's Press, 1982. 216p.

1469. Moscoff, W. "Part-time employment in the USSR." *Soviet Studies,* 34 (April 1982), 270-85.

1470. Matthews, M. "The "State Labour Reserves": an episode in Soviet social history." *Slavonic and East European Review,* 61 (April 1983), 238-51.

1471. Glickman, Rose L. *Russian factory women: workplace and society, 1880-1914.* Berkeley: University of California Press, 1984. 325p.

1472. Rutland, Peter. "The Shchekino method and the struggle to raise labour productivity in Soviet industry." *Soviet Studies,* 36 (July 1984),

345-65.

1473. Siline, A. "The new role of workers' collectives in the USSR." *International Labour Review*, 123, 6 (November-December 1984), 743-52.

See also 69, 74, 88, 123.

United Kingdom

1474. MacCafferty, Maxine (comp.) *Employment relations in the UK.* London: Aslib, 1976.

1475. Harrison, Royden, Woolven, Gillian B. and Duncan, Robert. *The Warwick guide to British labour periodicals 1790-1970.* Brighton: Harvester, 1977.

1476. Coates, Christine. *Trade unions and industrial relations.* London: The Library Association, 1978.

1477. Bain, George Sayers and Woolven, Gillian Beatrice (comps.) *A bibliography of British industrial relations.* Cambridge: Cambridge University Press, 1979.

Covers the period 1880-1970. Later supplements are listed below.

1478. Chell, E. and Rowat, C. *Worker participation: report and bibliography.* Emerson Rowat Information Services, 1979.

1479. Smart, Carol. *Industrial relations in Britain: a guide to sources of information.* London: Capital Planning Information, 1980.

1480. Walsh, Kenneth, Izzatt, Ann and Pearson, Richard. *The UK labour market: the IMS guide to information.* London: Kogan Page, 1980.

1481. Smith, Harold. *The British labour movement to 1970: a bibliography.* London: Mansell, 1981.

1482. Bennett, John (comp.) "Bibliography 1980." *British Journal of Industrial Relations*, 20, 3 (November 1982), 377-414.

Supplement to Bain and Woolven, 1979.

1483. Incomes Data Services. *Guide to sources of information.* London: I.D.S., 1982.

1484. Bennett, John (comp.) "Bibliography 1981." *British Journal of Industrial Relations*, 21, 2 (July 1983), 234-64.

Supplement to Bain and Woolven, 1979.

1485. Bennett, John (comp.) and Storey, Richard (ed.) *Trade union and related records.* Third edition. Coventry: University of Warwick Library, 1983.

1486. Winchester, David. "Industrial relations research in Britain." *British Journal of Industrial Relations,* 21, 1 (March 1983), 100-14.

Review of the current literature for the British Universities Industrial Relations Association.

1487. Bennett, John (comp.) "Bibliography 1982." *British Journal of Industrial Relations,* 22, 2 (July 1984), 218-64.

Supplement to Bain and Woolven, 1979.

1488. Bennett, John (comp.) "Bibliography 1983." *Society for the Study of Labour History Bulletin,* 48 (Spring 1984), 98-145.

This is the latest in a series of bibliographies published in the Spring issue of the Bulletin each year, covering British labour and social history. The first appeared in *Bulletin* 1 (Autumn 1960), 6-26.

1489. Bain, George Sayers and Bennett, John (comps.) *A bibliography of British industrial relations: a supplement 1971-1979.* Cambridge: Cambridge University Press, 1985.

Supplement to Bain and Woolven, 1979.

United States

1490. Committee of Industrial Relations Librarians. *Exchange bibliographies.* [A continuing series of short bibliographies on industrial relations topics with a subject index].

Author formerly entitled Committee of University Industrial Relations Librarians.

1491. Evansohn, John (and others). *Literature on the American working class.* New England Free Press, 1970.

1492. Kirkley, A. Roy. *Labor unions and the black experience: a selected bibliography.* Rutgers University, 1972.

1493. Soltow, Martha Jane, Forché, Carolyn and Massre, Murray. *Women in American labor history, 1825-1935: an annotated bibliography.* Michigan State University, School of Labor and Industrial Relations, 1972.

1494. McBrearty, James C. *American labor history and comparative labor movements: a selected bibliography.* University of Arizona Press, 1973.

1495. United States. Department of Labor. Library. *Library catalog of the ... Library.* New York: G. K. Hall, 1975. Thirty-eight volumes.

1496. Cornell University. New York State School of Industrial and Labor Relations. Library. *Library catalog of the ... Library.* New York: G. K. Hall, 1976. Twelve volumes.

First supplement, 1977.

Second supplement, 1978. Two volumes.

Third supplement, 1979. Two volumes.

Fourth supplement, 1980. Two volumes.

1497. Soltow, Martha Jane and Sokkar, J. A. S. *Industrial relations and personnel management: selected information sources.* New York: Scarecrow Press, 1979.

1498. Neufeld, Maurice F., Leab, Daniel J. and Swanson, Dorothy. *American working class history: a representative bibliography.* New York: Bowker, 1983.

1499. Dankert, Philip R. "Recent publications." *Industrial and Labor Relations Review*, 38, 2 (January 1985), 264-78.

This is the latest bibliography in a series published in each issue of the *Industrial and Labor Relations Review*. The first appeared in volume 1, number 1 (October 1947), 135-49.

Upper Volta

1500. Taylor, B."Democracy in Upper Volta." *Review of African Political Economy*, 21 (May-September 1981), 102-9.

1501. Wilcock, D. and Chuta, E. "Employment in rural indutries in Eastern Upper Volta." *International Labour Review*, 121, 4 (July-August 1982), 455-68.

Uruguay

1502. Pintos, F. R. *Historia del movimiento obrero del Uruguay.* Montevideo: Corporacion Grafica, 1960.

1503. Centro de Estudiantes de Ciencias y de Administracion *La empresa y la legislacion laboral.* Montevideo: C.E.C.A., 1962.

1504. Uruguayan Trade Union Confederation. "Fifth Ordinary Congress of the Uruguayan Trade Union Confederation." *International Labour Review*, 85, 2 (February 1962), 187-8.

West Indies

1505. United States. Bureau of Labor Statistics. *Labor law and practice in the Dominican Republic.* Washington: U.S.G.P.O., 1968. 39p.

1506. Tidrick, G. M. *Wages, output and the employment lag in Jamaica.* Williamstown: Williams College, Center for Development Economics, 1970.

1507. Elkan, W. and Morley, R. *Employment in a tourist economy: British Virgin Islands.* Durham: Durham University, Department of Economics, 1971. v 103p.

1508. International Labour Organisation. *Jamaica Productivity Centre: interim report on project results.* Geneva: I.L.O., 1971. 185p.

1509. Harewood, Jack (ed.) *Human resources in the Commonwealth Caribbean: report of a seminar.* Mona, Jamaica: University of the West Indies, 1972. 163p.

1510. Harrod, J. *Trade union foreign policy: a study of British and American trade union activities in Jamaica.* London: Macmillan, 1972. xiv, 485p.

1511. International Labour Organisation. *Employment and unemployment in Jamaica.* Geneva: I.L.O., 1972. iii, 149p.

1512. Thomas, Roy Darrow. *The adjustment of displaced workers in a labour surplus economy: a case study of Trinidad and Tobago.* Mona, Jamaica: University of the West Indies, 1972. 118p.

1513. Tidrick, G. M. *Wage spillover and unemployment in a wage gap economy: the Jamaican case.* Williamstown: Williams College, Center for Development Economics, 1972. 37p.

1514. Saadia, Y. *Report to the government of the Netherlands Antilles on workers' education.* Geneva: I.L.O., 1973. 21p.

1515. Elkin, H. S. *Netherlands Antilles: industrial relations, project findings and recommendations.* Geneva: I.L.O., 1974. 115p.

1516. International Labour Organisation. *Memorandum to the government of Montserrat on labour legislation and labour relations.* Geneva: I.L.O., 1974. 46p.

1517. Nicklin, L. H. *St. Kitts, Nevis and Anguilla: occupational safety and health.* Geneva: I.L.O., 1974. 19p.

1518. Summers, H. X. *Antigua: labour legislation.* Geneva: I.L.O., 1974.

114p.

1519. Johnson, C. L. "Political unionism and the collective objective in economies of British colonial origin: the cases of Jamaica and Trinidad." *American Journal of Economics and Sociology*, 34, 4 (October 1975), 365-80.

1520. Pazos, F. "Development and the underutilisation of labour: lessons of the Dominican Republic Employment Mission." *International Labour Review*, 113, 3 (March 1975), 235-49.

1521. Standing G. *Aspiration wages, migration and female employment.* Geneva: I.L.O., 1975. 25p.

1522. Tidrick, G. M. "Wage spillover and unemployment in a wage-gap economy: the Jamaican case." *Economic Development and Cultural Change*, 23, 2 (January 1975), 306-24.

1523. Agnihotri, V. *Grenada: manpower assessment and planning.* Geneva: I.L.O., 1976. 12p.

1524. Kritz, E. and Ramos, J. "Measurement of urban underemployment: a report on three experimental surveys." *International Labour Review*, 113, 1 (January-February 1976), 115-27.

Dominican Republic, Grenada and Jamaica.

1525. Robert, M. *St. Lucia: occupational safety and health.* Geneva: I.L.O., 1976.

1526. Lewis, William Arthur. *Labour in the West Indies: the birth of a workers' movement.* London: New Beacon Books, 1977. 104p.

1527. Johnson, C. L. "Emergence of political unionism in economies of British colonial origin: the cases of Jamaica and Trinidad." *American Journal of Economics and Sociology*, 39, 2 (April 1980), 151-67.

1528. Johnson, C. L. "Political unionism and autonomy in economies of British colonial origin: the cases of Jamaica and Trinidad." *American Journal of Economics and Sociology*, 39, 3 (July 1980), 237-48.

1529. Okpaluba, C. *Evolution of labour relations legislation in Trinidad and Tobago.* St. Augustine: University of the West Indies, Institute of Social and Economic Research, 1980. viii, 170p.

1530. Ennew, J. and Young, P. *Child labour in Jamaica: a general review.* London: Anti-Slavery Society, 1981. 75p.

1531. Standing, G. *Unemployment and female labour: a study of labour* *supply in Kingston, Jamaica.* London: Macmillan, 1981. xii, 364p.

1532. Williams, L. *Structure and operations of conciliation services in Trinidad and Tobago.* Geneva: I.L.O., 1981. 24p.

1533. International Labour Organisation." Report of the Commission of Inquiry ... [on] the observance of certain international labour conventions by the Dominican Republic and Haiti ..." *Official Bulletin (ILO),* 66, Special supplement B, (1983), 1-206.

1534. International Labour Organisation and Danish International Development Agency. *Mision preparatoria de seminario sub-regional Latinoamericano sobre "Desarrollo sindical co-operativo": informe final.* Geneva: I.L.O., 1983.

Dominican Republic.

1535. Ramdin, Ron. *From chattel slave to wage earner: a history of trade unionism in Trinidad and Tobago.* London: Martin Brian and O'Keefe, 1982. 314p.

1536. Richter, L. "Manpower and employment information through key informants." *International Labour Review,* 121, 4 (July-Auguat 1982), 417-31.

Includes Antigua.

See also 41, 133.

Yemen Arab Republic

1537. Allman, J. and Hill, A. "Fertility, migration and family planning in the Yemen Arab Republic." *Population Studies*, 32 (March 1978), 159-71.

1538. Birks, J. S., Sinclair, C. A. and Socknat, J. A. "Aspects of labour migration from North Yemen." *Middle Eastern Studies*, 17 (January 1981), 49-63.

Yugoslavia

1539. Kolaja, Jiri. *Workers' councils: the Yugoslav experience.* London: Tavistock, 1965. 84p.

1540. Adizes, I. *Industrial democracy, Yugoslav style: the effect of decentralisation on organisational behaviour.* New York: Free Press, 1971. xxi, 297p.

1541. Vanek, Jan. *The economics of workers' management: a Yugoslav case study.* London: Allen & Unwin, 1972. 315p.

1542. International Labour Organisation. Management Development Branch. "Workers' participation in Yugoslavia." *Management and Productivity*, 38 (1973), 46-51.

1543. Wachtel, Howard M. *Workers' management and workers' wages in Yugoslavia: the theory and practice of participatory socialism.* Cornell: Cornell University Press, 1973. 220p.

1544. Yugoslav Survey. "Conclusions of the Presidency of the League of Communists of Yugoslavia and the Presidency of the Socialist Federal Republic of Yugoslavia concerning the employment of Yugoslav nationals abroad and the execution of policy in this field." *Yugoslav Survey*, 14, 2 (May 1973), 39-44.

1545. Macura, M. "Employment problems under declining population growth rates and structural change: the case of Yugoslavia." *International Labour Review*, 109, 5-6 (May-June 1974), 487-501.

1546. Nikolic, M. "Employment and temporary unemployment." *Yugoslav Survey*, 14, 2 (May 1974), 1-22.

1547. Rozman, R. and Franc, V. *Planning in economic organisation in Yugoslavia.* Ljubljana: International Centre for Public Enterprises, 1974. 28p.

1548. Congdon, T. "Economics of industrial democracy." *New Society*, 34, 682 (30 October 1975), 255-7.

1549. Obradovic, J. "Workers' participation: who participates?" *Industrial Relations*, 14, 1 (February 1975), 32-44.

1550. Rasevic, M. *Determinants of labour force participation in Yugoslavia*. Geneva: I.L.O., 1975. 36p.

1551. Savez Sindikata Jugoslavije. "Confederation of Trade Unions Of Yugoslavia." *Yugoslav Survey*, 16, 2 (May 1975), 3-22.

1552. Obradovic, Josip and Dunn, William N. (eds.) *Workers' self-management and organisational power in Yugoslavia*. Pittsburgh: University of Pittsburgh, Center for International Studies, 1978. 448p.

1553. Comisso, Ellen Turkish. *Workers' control under plan and market: implications of Yugoslav self-management*. Yale: Yale University Press, 1979. 285p.

1554. Grozdanic, S. S. "Yugoslav workers' self-management: the recent trends, experience and perspectives." *Yugoslav Law*, 5, 3 (September-December 1979), 23-37.

1555. Sirc, L. *Yugoslav economy under self-management*. New York: St. Martin's Press, 1979. xix, 270p.

1556. Ardalan, C. "Workers' self-management and planning: the Yugoslav case." *World Development*, 8 (September 1980), 623-38.

1557. Seibel, H. D. and Damachi, U. G. *Self-management in Yugoslavia and the developing world*. London: Macmillan, 1980. 316p.

1558. Kavcic, B. *Recent trends in development of self-management in Yugoslavia*. Geneva: I.L.O., 1981. 18p.

1559. Kavcic, B. and Tannenbaum, A. S. "Longitudinal study of the distribution of control in Yugoslav organisations." *Human Relations*, 34, 5 (1981), 397-417.

1560. Pasic, M. *De l'autogestion ouvrière á l'organisation autogestionaire de la société*. Belgrade: Savez Sindikata Jugoslavije, 1981. 127p.

1561. Rosenberg, Richard D. and Rosenstein, Eliezer. "Operationalising workers' participation: a comparison of Yugoslavia and the USA." *Industrial Relations Journal*, 12, 2 (March-April 1981), 46-52.

1562. Schrenk, M. *Managerial structures and practices in* *manufacturing enterprises: a Yugoslav case study.* Washington: International Bank for Reconstruction and Development, 1981. iv, 100p.

1563. Estrin, S. "The effects of self-management on Yugoslav industrial growth." *Soviet Studies,* 34 (January 1982), 69-85.

1564. Pasic, Najdan, Grozdanic, Stanislav and Radevic, Milorad (eds.) *Workers' management in Yugoslavia: recent development and trends.* Geneva: I.L.O., 1982. 198p.

1565. Seibel, Hans Dieter and Damachi, Ukandi Godwin. *Self-management in Yugoslavia and the developing world.* London: Macmillan, 1982. vii, 316p.

1566. International Bank for Reconstruction and Development. *Yugoslavia: employment strategy and manpower policies for the 1980s.* Washington: I.B.R.D., 1983. ix, 129p.

1567. Milisavljevic, M. "Business planning and employee democracy in Yugoslavia." *Long Range Planning,* 16, 4 (August 1983), 84-9.

1568. Minev, D., Tominsek, A. and Dobrin, T. *Role of public enterprises in the advancement of women in Yugoslavia.* Ljubljana: International Centre for Public Enterprises in Developing Countries, 1983. 95p.

1569. Sacks, Stephen R. *Self-management and efficiency: large corporations in Yugoslavia.* London: Allen & Unwin, 1983. 163p.

See also 21, 29, 37, 57, 62, 96, 117.

Zaire

1570. Kazadi, W. A. and Dile, J. S. *Politiques salariales et développement en République Démocratique du Congo.* Paris: Editions Universitaires, 1970. xv, 478p.

1571. McCabe, J. L. *Employment in the Congo: a preliminary investigation.* New Haven: Yale University, Economic Growth Center, 1972. 31p.

1572. McCabe, J. L. *Unemployment as a social-welfare problem in urban Zaire.* New Haven: Yale University, Economic Growth Center, 1972. 27p.

1573. United States. Bureau of Labor Statistics. *Labor law and practice in the Republic of Zaire.* Washington: U.S.G.P.O., 1972. v, 85p.

1574. Fabian, J. "Kazi: conceptualizations of labor in a charismatic movement among Swahili-speaking workers." *Cahiers d'Etudes Africaines,* 13, 50 (1973), 293-325.

1575. Regional Economic Research and Documentation Center, Lome. *République du Zaire: legislation du travail: conventions collectives nationales.* Lome: The Centre, 1974.

1576. International Labour Organisation. *Zaire: planification des resources humaines: emploi et éducation.* Geneva: I.L.O., 1975. 19p.

1577. Gould, T. F. "New class of professional Zairian women." *African Review,* 7, 3-4 (1977), 92-105.

1578. Denys, M. M. "Quelques réflexions sur le régime juridique des conventions collectives au Zaire." *Penant,* 92, 776 (April-May 1982), 41-57.

See also 109.

Zambia

1579. Ohadike, Patrick O. *Development of and factors in the employment of African migrants in the copper mines of Zambia, 1940-66.* Manchester: Manchester University Press, 1969. 24p.

1580. Zambia. Central Statistical Office. *Employment and earnings, 1966-1968.* Lusaka: C.S.O., 1970. 50p.

1581. Clairmonte, F. F. *Zambia: wages, incomes and employment: an overview.* Stockholm: Universitet Stockholm, Institutet for

Internationell Ekonomi, 1971.

1582. Heisler, H. "The African workforce of Zambia." *Civilisations* 21, 4 (1971), 428-35.

1583. Jacobs, W. R. *The relationship between African trade unions and political organisations in Northern Rhodesia/Zambia, 1949-1961.* Geneva: International Institute for Labour Studies, 1971. 30p.

1584. Burawoy, M. "Another look at the mineworker." *African Social Research*, 14 (December 1972), 239-87.

1585. Ghadike, P. "Bottlenecks in the Zambian labour situation." *Journal of Administration Overseas*, 11, 4 (October 1972), 260-72.

1586. Kapferer, B. *Strategy and transaction in an African factory: African workers and Indian management in a Zambian town.* Manchester: Manchester University Press, 1972. xxii, 366p.

1587. Naranza, J. N. *Modern sector employment growth in East Africa with special emphasis on Zambia.* Ithaca: Cornell University, 1973. xiv, 208p.

1588. Zambia Congress of Trade Unions. *Report of the working party appointed by the General Council to enquire into the structure of trade unions in Zambia.* Kitwe: Z.C.T.U., 1973. 101p.

1589. Burawoy, M. *Constraint and manipulation in industrial conflict: a comparison of strikes among Zambian workers in a clothing factory and the mining industry.* Lusaka: Zambia University, Institute for African Studies, 1974. 57p.

1590. Harries-Jones, Peter. *Freedom and labour: mobilization and political control on the Zambian copperbelt.* Oxford: Blackwell, 1975. 256p.

1591. Zambia. Commission of Inquiry into the salaries, salary structures and conditions of service of the Zambia public and teaching services. *Report of the Commission ...* Lusaka: The Commission, 1975.

1592. Nguvu, M. B. N. *Role of trade unions and employers' associations in socio-economic development and employment promotion in Zambia.* Geneva: International Institute for Labour Studies, 1976. 27p.

1593. Daniel, Philip. *Africanisation, nationalisation and inequality: mining labour and the copperbelt in Zambian development.* Cambridge: Cambridge University Press, 1979. 202p.

1594. Fincham, R. *Employment in Zambia.* Lusaka: Zambia University, School of Humanities and Social Sciences, 1979. 129p.

1595. Fry, James. *Employment and income distribution in the African economy.* London: Croom Helm, 1979. 186p.

1596. Koloko. M. E. *Manpower approach to planning: theoretical issues and evidence from Zambia.* Denver: Denver University, Graduate School of International Studies, 1980. xvi, 94p.

1597. Todd, D. M. and Shaw, C. "The informal sector and Zambia's employment crisis." *Journal of Modern African Studies,* 18 (September 1980), 411-25.

1598. Zambia Congress of Trade Unions. *Constitution of the* ... Kitwe: Z.C.T.U., 1980. 43p.

1599. Chiburesha, E. *Employee participation in decision making within the undertaking.* Geneva: I.L.O., 1981.

1600. Mwamba. F. M. *Workers' participation in management in Zambia.* Geneva: I.L.O., 1981. 5p.

1601. Tenthani, E. M. *Workers' participation in decisions within undertakings in Zambia.* Geneva: I.L.O., 1981. 2p.

1602. International Labour Organisation. *Report of the National Tripartite Seminar on the Development of Labour Relations in Zambia, Lusaka, 1980.* Geneva: I.L.O., 1982. 11p.

1603. Perrings, C. "Premise and inference in labour studies: a Zambian example." *African Affairs,* 81 (January 1982), 87-99.

1604. International Labour Organisation. *Technical memorandum to the government of Zambia on a mission to advise on the functioning of the works council system.* Geneva: I.L.O., 1983. ii, 18p.

1605. International Labour Organisation. *Technical memorandum to the government of Zambia on a mission to advise on the preparation of self-management experiments in pilot enterprises.* Geneva: I.L.O., 1983. 35p.

1606. Pottier, Johan. "Defunct labour reserve? Mambwe villages in the post-migration economy." *Africa,* 53, 2 (1983), 2-23.

See also 32, 41, 110, 144, 147.

Zimbabwe

1607. Clarke, D. G. *Domestic workers in Rhodesia: the economics of masters and servants.* Gwelo: Mambo Press, 1974. 88p.

1608. Harris, P. S. "Industrial relations in Rhodesia." *South African Journal of Economics*, 42, 1 (March 1974), 65-84.

1609. Rhodesia. Central Statistical Office. *Census of production 1972/73: mining, manufacturing, construction, electricity and water supply.* Salisbury: C.S.O., 1974. 116p.

   Includes some labour statistics.

1610. Harris, P. "Industrial workers in Rhodesia, 1946-1972: working-class elites or lumpenproletariat?" *Journal of Southern African Studies*, 1, 2 (April 1975), 139-61.

1611. Van Onselen, C. "Black workers in Central African industry: a critical essay on the historiography and sociology of Rhodesia." *Journal of Southern African Studies*, 1, 2 (April 1975), 228-46.

1612. Van Onselen, C. *Chibaro: African mine labour in Southern Rhodesia 1900-1933.* London: Pluto Press, 1976. 326p.

1613. Fauber, S. A. "Minimum wage legislation in dveloping countries: Zimbabwe, a case in point." *Journal of International Law*, 13, 2 (Spring 1981), 385-411.

1614. Mortimer, Jim. "The challenges facing Zimbabwe." *Personnel Management*, 13, 11 (November 1981), 43-5.

1615. Riddell, R. C. *Report of the Commission of Inquiry into incomes, prices and conditions of service.* Salisbury: Government Printer, 1981. ii, 330p.

1616. Muir, K. A., Blackie. M. J., Kinsey, B. H. and De Swardt, M. L. A. "Employment effects of 1980 price and wage policy in the Zimbabwe maize and tobacco industries." *African Affairs*, 81, 322 (January 1982), 71-85.

1617. Garvin, R. T. "Management of labour on Zimbabwe flue-cured tobacco farms: quo vadis?" *Agricultural Administration*, 12, 4 (April 1983), 195-206.

1618. Matshazi, M. J. and Tillfors, C. *Survey of workers' education activities in Zimbabwe, 1980-1981.* Uppsala: Nardiska Afrikainstitutet, 1983. 85p.

1619. King, F. J. *Zimbabwe: National Manpower Survey: terminal report.* Harare: I.L.O., 1984. 43p.

See also 22, 87, 110, 147.

Author index

Moss, Bernard H. 521
Mouly, J. 733
Moyo, Nelson 324
Muir, J. D. 798
Muir, K. A. 1616
Mujahid, G. B. S. 793
Mulat, T. 1333
Müller-Jentsch, Walter 568, 571, 575
Mulvey, Charles 801
Mumford, Enid 72
Munch-Peterson, P. M. 891
Mundle, S. 149
Munim, M. A. 1102
Murg, Gary E. 61
Murugasu, Sheila 1218
Mustafa, M. M. 1329
Mutatkar, V. A. 669
Mutrushi, Vasil 172
Muzumdar, D. 895
Mwamba, F. M. 1600
Myrdal, H. G.

Nagi, M. H. 480, 482
Nair, A. 849
Nakao, T. 772
Naranza, J. N. 1587
Nash, June 318
Nass, Gabriele 577
Naasar, S. Z. 483
Natchaba, C. F. 1405
Natesan, V. R. 669
National Trades Union Congress (Singapore) 1199
National Tripartite Seminar on the Improvement of Working Conditions and Environment in Sri Lanka 1317
National Union of Mineworkers (UK) 317, 319
Nave-Herz, R. 5
Navratil, O. 433

Nazumdar, D. 908
Nbim, S. M. 586
Nellis, John R. 185, 186
Nelson, D. 1180
Ner, A. B. 62
Neuberger, E. 62
Neufeld, Maurice F. 1498
Nevin, Donal 697
Newman, Peter 622
Nguvu, M. B. N. 1592
Nicholls, D. 626
Nicklin, L. H. 1517
Nielsen, Birthe 448
Nielsen, L. 454
Nigeria. National Manpower Board 1015, 1016, 1017, 1024
Nijhar, K. S. 882
Nikolic, M. 1546
Nikon, Keizai 749
Niland, John 203, 213, 227, 229
Nishiyama, Shunsaitu 773
Nogues, J. 198
Nolan, Peter 398
Norway. Arbeidsdirektoratet 1053
Norway. Arbeidstilsynet 1071
Norway. Direktoratet for Arbeidstilsynet 1063
Norway. Komiteen for Internasjonale Sosialpolitisker Saker 1054
Norway. Kommunal og Arbeidsdepartment 1064
Norway. Statistisk Sentralbyra 1072
Norwood, Janet L. 348
Nouga, Adelbert 350
Nove, Alec 1464
Nwabueze, R. O. 1035
Nwanza, Z. M. 19
Nygaard, K. 1055, 1065

Subject index

Immigration 530, 531, 588, 622, 827, 1079, 1183

Incentives 1176, 1463

Income distribution 28, 98, 115, 141, 170, 197, 334, 336, 398, 403, 413, 490, 655, 659, 700, 768, 802, 805, 808, 845, 908, 920, 1342, 1429, 1457, 1593, 1595

Incomes 156, 201, 218, 259, 294, 389, 391, 412, 434, 436, 465, 470, 526, 543, 584, 566, 617, 729, 734, 736, 768, 772, 791, 801, 804, 811, 825, 922, 926, 934, 1076, 1167, 1261, 1312, 1336, 1360, 1387, 1389, 1427, 1483, 1506, 1513, 1521, 1522, 1543, 1580, 1581, 1591, 1615

Incomes policy 69, 80, 95, 130, 215, 236, 302, 324, 470, 504, 511, 650, 670, 688, 709, 833, 854, 918, 978, 1007, 1058, 1142, 1181, 1212, 1357, 1420, 1447, 1570, 1616

India 25, 82, 106, 111, 112, 117, 128, 133, 149, 647-65

Indonesia 31, 145, 149, 666-84

Industrial conflict 11, 53, 56, 142, 150, 176, 221, 225, 300, 312, 335, 358, 363, 379, 394, 477, 529, 538, 541, 561, 575, 601, 639, 714, 715, 717, 718, 749, 783, 798, 879, 904, 912, 931, 952, 991, 1033, 1041, 1084, 1131, 1161, 1245, 1259, 1263, 1275, 1347, 1353, 1439, 1452, 1459

International labour conventions 26, 147, 193, 285, 340, 836, 968, 1221, 1374, 1375, 1441, 1533

International trade unions 30, 93, 94, 143, 210

Iran 25, 35, 685-91

Iraq 692-3

Ireland 80, 694-707

Israel 21, 29, 62, 86, 130, 708-15

Italy 14, 21, 52, 136, 140, 716-23

Ivory Coast 28, 724-39

Jamaica *See* West Indies. *See also* 1506, 1508, 1510, 1511, 1513, 1519, 1520, 1522, 1524, 1527, 1528, 1530, 1531

Japan 23, 90, 134, 149, 740-90, 1399

Job satisfaction 700, 1459

Jordan 26, 791-4

Kenya 19, 98, 108, 110, 112, 795-808

Korea, North 809-22

Korea, South 24, 120, 823-6

Kuwait 827

Labour economics 203, 555, 766, 976, 979, 1382, 1541, 1548, 1555, 1563, 1607

Labour history 165, 194, 210, 216, 231, 316, 333, 341, 342, 358, 376, 395, 410, 513, 516, 521, 535, 556, 600, 629, 695, 703, 704, 708, 717, 718, 719, 797, 874, 879, 886, 893, 923, 950, 969, 986, 1169, 1233, 1235, 1250, 1257, 1272, 1364, 1414, 1415, 1454, 1456, 1467, 1470, 1471, 1475, 1481, 1485, 1488, 1491, 1493, 1494, 1498, 1502, 1526, 1535, 1610,